D1007672

To Catch
a Cat

Green, Heather, 1967-
To catch a cat : how
three stray kittens resc
2016.
33305236666867
gi   12/28/16

To Catch a Cat

How Three Stray Kittens Rescued Me

HEATHER GREEN

BERKLEY BOOKS, NEW YORK

BERKLEY

An imprint of Penguin Random House LLC
375 Hudson Street, New York, New York 10014

This book is an original publication of Penguin Random House LLC.

Copyright © 2016 by Heather Green.
Penguin supports copyright. Copyright fuels creativity, encourages diverse voices,
promotes free speech, and creates a vibrant culture. Thank you for buying an authorized
edition of this book and for complying with copyright laws by not reproducing, scanning, or
distributing any part of it in any form without permission. You are supporting writers and
allowing Penguin to continue to publish books for every reader.

BERKLEY® and the "B" design are registered trademarks of Penguin Random House LLC.
For more information, visit penguin.com.

Library of Congress Cataloging-in-Publication Data

Names: Green, Heather, 1967–, author.
Title: To catch a cat : how three stray kittens rescued me / by Heather Green.
Description: Berkley trade paperback edition. I New York : Berkley Books, 2016.
Identifiers: LCCN 2016005368 (print) I LCCN 2016020405 (ebook) I
ISBN 9780425281987 I ISBN 9780698197978 ()
Subjects: LCSH: Feral cats—New Jersey—Union City—Anecdotes. I
Cat rescue—New Jersey—Union City—Anecdotes. I Kittens—
New Jersey—Union City—Anecdotes. I Green, Heather, 1967–
Classification: LCC SF450 .G74 2016 (print) I LCC SF450 (ebook) I DDC
636.8/0709749—dc23
LC record available at https://lccn.loc.gov/2016005368

PUBLISHING HISTORY
Berkley trade paperback edition / July 2016

PRINTED IN THE UNITED STATES OF AMERICA

10 9 8 7 6 5 4 3 2 1

Cover design by Judith Murello.
Interior text design by Laura K. Corless.
Author photo © by Matthew P. Greer.

Some names and identifying characteristics have been changed to protect
the privacy of the individuals involved.

Most Berkley Books are available at special quantity discounts for bulk purchases for sales,
promotions, premiums, fund-raising, or educational use. Special books, or book excerpts, can also
be created to fit specific needs. For details, write: specialmarkets@penguinrandomhouse.com.

Penguin is committed to publishing works of quality and integrity.
In that spirit, we are proud to offer this book to our readers;
however, the story, the experiences, and the words
are the author's alone.

Penguin
Random
House

For Lily, after all

Acknowledgments

I never thought I'd write a book. I'm a business writer by training. But I knew I'd never have the patience to spend months chronicling the rise (or fall) of the latest tech titan and how their entrepreneurial bent was clear from the first lemonade stand they ran at age four. (There's always a lemonade stand . . .) And then along came some kittens.

Still, nothing I typed would have amounted to much without the help and encouragement of a crowd of people. Starting with my agent, Lindsay Edgecombe at Levine Greenberg Rostan Literary Agency. My book may be about cute, tumbling kittens, but Lindsay is savvy, smart, and practical—exactly the foil I needed. Lindsay helped me shape and sharpen my book so it could become more than just a tale about rescuing cats. She and Stephanie Rostan, who first signed me, encouraged me to keep writing when my first attempts missed the mark, believing in my story and our ability to work together to create something a broad audience could connect with. Lindsay is the agent for today's world, committed to working on every aspect of a book, from story arc to marketing, with a deft and true literary eye.

Acknowledgments

I am incredibly grateful to Allison Janice, my editor at the Berkley Publishing Group, who believed in my cat story and who improved it with thoughtful insight. Allison was patient when I most needed understanding and ready to attack when the book needed it. The best editor is the one who can help you figure out how to get on the page what's in your head, all in your own words. Allison is that kind of an editor. She is a dedicated, smart, and devoted reader. I knew from the very first notes she gave me that I was lucky to be working with her and the folks at Berkley. I appreciate the chance she and Berkley gave me to share this story and to bring out the best in this book.

A big thank-you and lots of kitty emojis to my cat people. It takes a village—or many villages, including Jersey City, Hoboken, Weehawken, and Union City. Jersey Strong! (I *never* thought I'd say that.) Carol McNichol at Companion Animal Trust and Patty Drumgoole, Hoboken rescuer extraordinaire, are the toughest rescuers I know. You represent the front lines to me and I'll never understand how you keep going strong despite the heartache. I love your resilience, your take-no-prisoners attitude, and your deep empathy. Joan Doljan truly is a diplomat who plainly sees the faults in humans, but also their well-meaning desire to do what they can for cats. Robin Murphy at Companion Animal Placement is directly responsible for saving the lives and improving the well-being of so many cats and easing the burden of so many rescuers. Beverly Parsons at Jersey Cats, thank you for every time you said yes to taking on one more of our cats and finding them wonderful homes. You made it possible for us to rescue so many more. Veena Prakash, your doggedness and clear-eyed

Acknowledgments

understanding of people helps you navigate the complicated world of rescue groups so that you can help our Union City kitties. Erica Huddy, you ushered me back into a second round of cat rescuing after Lily was born through your compassion, your strong will, and your ability to get things done. Athina Glindmeyer, I adore your optimism, energy, humor, and entrepreneurial spirit. Shout-out to Rukas the cat! I still don't understand how, without an opposable thumb, you manage to crochet all those bow ties.

I'm especially thankful, however, to Alisha Smilovitz. Alisha, you're the most clear-eyed, big-hearted, irreverent cat rescuer I ever had the pleasure to know. The compassion you bring to understanding people and cats taught me so much about cats, other people, and myself. You are patient, intelligent, and kind. I am grateful to know you. I am also grateful that Carol McNichol and Mike Phillips brought Jean Long into my life. Jean, every day you throw yourself back into the fray, facing the saddest task there is in the rescue world. Thank you for your friendship and patience.

I'm lucky to have Steve Baker, remarkable writer and globetrotter extraordinaire, as a friend and a first reader. Your encouragement that I should write a book and your example in throwing yourself into publishing inspired me. Your suggestions and line edits were immensely helpful, but it was just your overall optimism and faith that inspired me. Thank you as well to Alice Peck for all the hard work and guidance you gave me in helping me rethink my book and believe in it again.

A huge thanks to my dear friends Debra Sparks, Mara Der Hovanesian, Debbie Becher, Jennifer Weil, Tevis Trower, and Alex

Acknowledgments

Walker, who listened to me as I tried to work out different pieces of this story; read *many, many* different versions of this book; and just generally had my back. I owe every one of you a drink.

I am immensely grateful to my parents, Carolyn and Bud Green. You both taught me what commitment to family means (though it took me long enough to apply that to my own little trio!). Dad, one of my strongest memories from childhood is you sitting on the kitchen stairs at the farm when I was in middle school, intently reading some of my earnest poems and saying how great you thought they were. Your interest and pride in what I was thinking and feeling gave me the room to think I could do anything. Mommy dearest, you are always there for me and you support me no matter what. Knowing that made it possible for me to try so many things. Thank you for that kind of love and the appreciation you taught me for finding a voice in writing, which I see in everything you write.

I am so lucky to have my daughter, Lily, in my life. (It's Lilly on her birth certificate, but Lily in her heart.) Lily is a cat whisperer who helped to tame countless kittens through her patience and curiosity. Lily's funny, compassionate, eager view on things inspires me. An entirely new life opened up for me when we had her.

Finally Matt, I can't believe you didn't want me to do an acknowledgment section! Who do I have to thank but you? All those times you jumped over a fence to trap a cat, the countless cages you cleaned, all that ferrying around of cats, the worry we shared, the scheming and planning, the taming of kitten after kitten. I know I will spend my life learning how to be part of a couple and I will make many more mistakes. But with you, I learned that, of course, nothing is perfect. You can always try something another way. The key is to try, to focus on the good around us. Even a cynical girl can learn a thing or two about trust.

1

Just a Few Kittens

As I stared over the backyard fence of my boyfriend Matt's house in Union City, New Jersey, what struck me was just how much mayhem you could pack into a postage stamp–sized patio.

In the overgrown yard next door, Matt's neighbor Roberto was doing an awkward dance, hopping from one foot to the other as he swung a battered machete in a semicircle, attempting to create a safe space between himself and some movement he thought he had spotted in the weeds. Matt was standing just outside the arc of the knife's reach, trying to calm Roberto down and jumping back every time the big man made another wild turn.

I craned forward, leaning against the sun-warmed wooden planks of the fence that separated Matt's yard from his neighbor's to get a better look.

"There's one!" Roberto yelled in a high-pitched, squeaking voice that undercut his tough-guy appearance. He thrust his machete in the direction of a small black-and-white body that darted out from its hiding place inside a weathered tire. I jerked back, but I didn't need to worry. The only object at risk of getting whacked was a pink hibiscus flower swaying on a branch above his shoulder. The ball of fur on the ground feinted to the left and then jumped to the right, disappearing behind the metal shed in the corner of the yard.

"See, Roberto, it's like I told you," Matt yelled. "Those are kittens!"

Our kitten-napping plans were going up in smoke, done in by an impromptu barbeque.

That black-and-white blur was indeed a wild kitten we had named Zero, one of a litter of three that Matt and I had been plotting to rescue in a couple of weeks. At least, until Roberto had walked into his backyard for the first time ever, towing a deflated pink kiddie pool, a machete, and a boom box big enough to be straight from the 1980s, intent on this fine June Saturday on having a cookout in the unkempt yard of the house he rented next to Matt. The machete was for cutting weeds. I hoped.

What Matt's neighbor was just discovering was something my boyfriend and I had also recently learned—that a trio of kittens called Roberto's patio home. We'd spotted the babies two weeks ago over the fence, amazed to see them trundling around. They moved fast, but since they were small, they didn't cover much ground. The littermates, who Matt soon dubbed Number

Three, Two Spot, and Zero in honor of their spots (or lack of them), weren't lost. They were four-week-old wild kittens learning to master their limbs and their nursery, this neglected backyard strewn with rotting wooden doors, rusting paint cans, and old newspapers. Their mother, a tidy, nearly all-white beauty who Matt dubbed Oona, showed up throughout the day to check on them, nurse them, and restore their coats, dirty from hours of play, to a glossy shine through meticulous, ruthless licking.

The moment I saw them I knew we would save them. Never mind, or maybe because of, the fact I'd never rescued a cat in my life or that my track record in committing myself to causes was spotty. I can guarantee that Matt never saw any of this coming when he'd moved to Union City, New Jersey, from Manhattan two years earlier, having found in this forgotten city's worn-down streets a place where he could just be. Matt, tall with calm, deep-set eyes and his deliberate way of walking, is a contemplator. He isn't so much a loner as someone who appreciates immersing himself fully into singular pursuits—like caring for a few thousand bees on his roof. Not that Matt is some reserved intellectual. His favorite Saturday ritual is sitting at a silver Formica kitchen table he inherited from his grandmother, reading the paper while listening to NPR's *Car Talk* and giggling uncontrollably in great bursts. *America's Funniest Home Videos*, *National Lampoon's Vacation*, Matt can't contain himself when it comes to slapstick.

Though he might have a solitary vein, Matt's good-natured willingness to help makes him the guy who steps forward to give a hand to a mother lugging a stroller up the subway stairs, or who gets up to give his seat to an elderly person on the bus (though, being independent New Yorkers, they often tartly respond that they don't *need* the seat, please sit down, young man). Even his bee project was prompted by wanting to join others in preventing pollinator populations from collapsing. Which is why, after finding the kittens, he'd allowed himself to be dragged into my scheme and agreed to help me map out an intricate strategy for rescuing them, one full of stealthy moves, smelly tuna, and a well-placed trap. Yet, as we were novices to the world of cat trapping, we'd forgotten one key step. Namely, letting Roberto in on our cat-napping schemes and asking him whether he would mind leaving the kittens alone while we made preparations.

That rookie move was why, weeks ahead of our planned cat-napping D-day, all hell was breaking loose.

Matt and I were on the roof watering a vegetable garden we'd planted in some raised beds when we got the first inkling that things were not as they should be. When I heard a rhythmic thwacking downstairs, I peeked over the edge, shocked to see anyone in one of the courtyards behind the row houses on Matt's block. No one ever went into these backyards. They were an abandoned land of forgotten junk. Which is likely the reason why Oona, the kittens' mother, had set up house there.

That's when I spotted Roberto down below. Matt came over to stand next to me and peer over the edge of the roof just as

Roberto lifted up the old wooden door on the ground that the kittens often hid under. Out scooted Two Spot, the brother who bravely followed but never led. Now, he was on his own. With a lunge and a blur of tiny legs, the little animal dove into the patch of tall grass flourishing next to a row of rotted-out gutters leaning against the far wall and disappeared. Roberto jumped back, dropping the door.

"Aie!" he cried in an inarticulate heave of fear, shaking his machete for good measure. Roberto was a compact brick of a man. Yet, on top of all that bulk was the softest, roundest face possible, exactly the picture you would expect to see on the front of a baby food jar, if the baby had a mustache. This was also the face that, on occasion, launched police cruisers into the night toward Matt's residential street, lighting it up with ice blue lights on a regular basis for playing loud music at two in the morning or threatening a fight with his neighbor. I would never have suspected that a few little balls of fluff would undo Roberto's chubby-cheeked Latino machismo.

Matt sprinted across the black tar roof and down the ladder. By the time I made it out back, he'd pulled Roberto to the side of the yard. I caught the end of Matt's out-of-breath explanation.

". . . kittens back here we've been taking care of."

"There's more?" Roberto squeaked. "Sure they aren't rats? They look like rats. Small, fast."

"It's three kittens," Matt explained, hesitating a moment. Matt's a scientist underneath it all. He likes precise descriptions, not a flood of words. Which means he starts and stops often when he's trying to explain something important. Listening to him is a bit like watching a stone skipping across a lake in slow motion, the rock rising and falling slowly in silence until the next punctuation of sound. You need patience, which I don't always have. I studied Roberto to see if he would hang on for the ride.

"Could you wait, do you think?" Matt paused. "We want to catch them in a couple of weekends." Another silence.

Roberto responded in a rush. "No, man. I work two jobs. I never have time off. I'm up early and back late. Today I'm off and I'm taking it easy. I'm cleaning this place up, having a beer, and blowing up a pool so my baby can go swimming." He stared hard at Matt, warding off any comments he might make about the pink inflatable pool lying a few feet away.

"I get it," Matt said in a thoughtful tone that made Roberto lower his shoulders just the slightest bit.

Matt looked off, working out the problem. Then in a fast staccato that matched Roberto's, he switched gears. "I'll help you move the door out of the way."

If ever Matt wanted to change professions, I was beginning to think that hostage negotiator might be a good fit.

Roberto gazed around. The tone had shifted. He wasn't being told to stop, just asked if he could change his plan a bit, with the added bonus of some help. In a short time, he had managed to clear out a good-sized square of the concrete patio. But there was still some junk piled up along the edges of the fence and in the back of the yard that needed moving.

"What's the big deal about kittens?" he asked, holding on to an edge of suspicion that there had to be more here than Matt was letting on. Matt's neighborhood was overrun with cats. Stray felines were as common in Union City as the slim plastic Virgin Mary statues that you spotted in front of every third house, a tiny blue lady on guard in a half-dome clamshell, clasping her hands in prayer while managing to monitor your every move. That is to say, cats were rampant—trotting across busy streets, hanging out behind corner grocery stores, skulking through backyards. Here and there you would spot aluminum take-out trays with food on a stoop, but most people didn't give the animals a second thought.

"They're little," Matt explained, holding his hands about six inches apart from each other. "My girlfriend feels bad for them. She wants to take them in."

He glanced over at me with his broad blue eyes just in time to catch me rolling mine. Did my careful-about-every-word boyfriend just invoke the girlfriend cliché?

But Matt was better at playing to the crowd than I imagined, because Roberto was nodding as if everything now made perfect sense.

"They won't hurt you," Matt added. "They're just looking for a place to hide."

Roberto shot a look over at me, worried I might think he was scared of a few kittens. "Oh yeah," he agreed, as if savvy to the ways of young cats.

That was how clever Matt talked Roberto into letting him help. Not that Roberto was completely convinced. He still thought Matt might be harboring rats. While Matt walked with slow, watchful steps, moving pieces of wood with the careful precision of the architect he was, so he wouldn't startle the kittens or hurt them, Roberto was eager to create a safe, animal-free zone around himself. He jettisoned buckets and bits of metal into the far corner with rapid heaves and tromped around without looking where he was going.

The inevitable was bound to happen again and did—twice. The first time was when Roberto's wild, machete-swinging dance flushed out Zero and he screamed "There's one!" He had the proof he needed now. Just as Matt had said, we were dealing in baby cats, not rats. Without a glance at either of us, Roberto walked over to the back side of his house and laid down his machete.

Not five minutes later, Roberto reached down and gave a bright blue plastic tarp lying on the ground a jerk, and yet another small body shot out, as if catapulted. Number Three launched forward, heading for the ten-foot-high concrete wall straight ahead of him. This was a classic Number Three move: when in doubt, throw yourself at the closest object. Despite his low odds of scaling a wall ten times taller than his body stretched out, Number Three tried, his paws scrabbling back and forth, before his body slid back down, right into Matt's outstretched hands. The kitten gave a hiss and a desperate heave before Matt managed to pull out the pillowcase he had shoved into his jeans pocket and thrust the wriggling mass of fur inside.

A spectacular catch. One that once and for all killed off any hope of getting the other two because it triggered the loudest yell from Roberto yet. No living creature would dare come out after that scream.

Matt walked over to me with the kitten-filled pillowcase.

"Roberto is freaked out," Matt said, shaking his head in amazement as he handed the bag over to me. "You can handle Number Three, right?"

I tilted my head forward in agreement, but I wasn't so sure. I liked plans, and what was unfolding here was a crazy sequence of events. I didn't say anything, but it was as if Matt heard me clear as day. Before disappearing behind the fence again to help clean up and keep Roberto from doing further damage, he rattled off a few sentences: "Take Number Three inside. Find a dark space for him. Keep everything quiet. Try to stay calm."

I stared for a minute at the empty space in front of me, befuddled by that remarkable and commanding set of instructions. Remarkable because that decisive guy, that wasn't my boyfriend. My boyfriend was not the give-orders type. He was more the listening, nodding, understanding-what-other-people-are-going-through breed.

Weird things were happening.

Three tiny kittens, born just six weeks ago, were already turning a bunch of humans upside down.

It had all started two weeks earlier.

Teevee found the kittens. Teevee was a demure tabby with the face of a dolphin who Matt had adopted, along with her brother Radio, years before I met him. Unlike me, Matt deliberates, he takes his time. He spent a few months looking for just the right companions, visiting shelters up and down the island of Manhattan almost every weekend, gazing at cats, holding their bodies next to his, dodging claws, sometimes not very well. Then one afternoon, Matt spotted Teevee huddling behind her bolder brother in a metal cage at the ASPCA. He decided there and then that this odd couple was exactly what his life needed. Matt is methodical, programming his phone to alert him when to take his vitamins, but he is only absentmindedly part of this world. He arranges his bills into piles and then forgets about them so completely that he's surprised when second and then collection notices show up. Matt's distractedness is why I'm shocked and inspired by how he embraces something when it strikes him as right, even though he may be uncertain how it is going to work out.

The kitten discovery happened on a rare, fateful Saturday morning that I was spending at Matt's place in New Jersey. I say rare because Matt spent most weekends with me at my apartment in New York City on the Upper West Side. During the workweek, we both returned to our respective corners: mine in Manhattan, his in New Jersey. But that weekend was different. I had made an unprecedented visit to his house just to prove that I could make sacrifices as his girlfriend—though I planned to space out my weekends in Union City *a lot*. Because people in New Jersey only laugh halfheartedly when they explain where they live based on the nearest Turnpike exit. Tying key details of my life to a highway that winds through industrial wastelands wasn't exactly a change I was eager to make. Where did it end? Saying motz instead of mozzarella? Suburbia?

No way. Busy, brash, appropriately neurotic cities—that was the life for me. Meeting up with friends for a late-morning brunch inside the Metropolitan Museum, lying out on a blanket in a tucked-away garden in Central Park, watching Shakespeare under the stars in the open-air Delacorte Theatre next to the Great Lawn. There was nothing like a summer weekend on the Upper West Side.

I went downstairs in the Union City house and was greeted by Matt handing me a cup of coffee.

"You'll never guess what Teevee found," he said.

I looked outside at Matt's backyard and was shocked to see Teevee pacing along the cement half of the fence that separated Matt's patio from his neighbor's. Teevee never stayed out in the open. She was a scrouncher of a cat, the kind that presses herself hard against the side of the wall when she encounters you in the hallway, hoping she has become invisible. Except here she was up on the wall, patrolling whatever it was that she had uncovered on the other side.

"Go on, climb up on that chair and you'll see."

I walked outside. It was the first weekend of June, but the end of spring was hanging on, the sunlight balancing lightly on a cool breeze. Nothing happened except that Teevee inched away from me. I peered over the concrete wall into the next-door neighbor's little backyard and saw what I had come to expect to see in Union City—a lot of old junk: rusting paint cans, scraggly mile-a-minute weeds growing up around a lone white plastic chair, a haphazard grouping of old kids' bikes. Bits and pieces discarded as people moved in and out, either because they thought nothing of dumping them or didn't have time to cram them into the truck as they fled the rental building, driven away by lack of money, an old boyfriend, a lost job.

That was all I noticed. I gazed back at Matt, who was flipping pancakes in the kitchen. Few things make Matt happier than losing himself in novel sweet breakfast concoctions. As I was about to step down, I saw them out of the corner of my eye. At first, they looked a lot like Tribbles from *Star Trek*. The three kittens were so low to the ground that you couldn't make out their minuscule legs. They were black-and-white, tiny little puffballs scooting around the yard, or rather, one part of the yard. Despite their surroundings, the piles of old newspaper, the rotting pieces of wood, even the bits of broken glass, they were scrubbed clean, a well-tended litter.

One of the balls of fur ping-ponging around the lot looked up, spotted me, and stopped his patrolling. I waited for him to realize just how gigantic, how foreign, how hairless I was and scoot off. Instead he did something that I later learned was typical of this fellow, who we would name Number Three. He cocked his oversized head to the left, put one careful paw in front of the other, and, as if he was still learning to defy gravity with baby steps, started walking toward me, his small white chest out, his golden eyes never leaving me.

It was the first time Number Three ever saw a human. This guy, all two pounds of him, was pure bravado. He sat down, settling his hind legs onto a pile of dry leaves. He was no bigger than my hand, his gigantic eyes taking up a quarter of his body. We stared at each other for another minute. He was confident, at home in his backyard world, tilting his head, trying to figure out if I was something he could play with. Because that was Number Three's reason for being—playing, jumping, and rolling. (Also destroying hosta plants, as would soon become apparent.) Then, one of his siblings tumbled through a gap in the tall grass and crashed into him. They fell back, a tangle of legs and paws and black-and-white fur, until, just as suddenly, they both jumped up and disappeared behind the metal shed.

Ferals are weird oddities. They inhabit a parallel world of lost things that I had never before given a second thought. I had seen wild kittens before, skulking in the shadows of a dairy barn near my parents' house when I was growing up, darting across the hot pavement of Alice Street in Waycross, Georgia, where my grandmother lived. I noticed them since they resembled the house cats I grew up with. But I never recognized them, because they were aloof and lived an alien life.

Now, Number Three had looked right at me. I had looked back. We had seen each other. In a distracted age where everything whizzes by, I realized how different what just happened was. I'd spent hours in yoga, focusing on controlling the air coming in and out of my nose, wrangling my legs and arms just so, sweating hard, trying to relax and just connect, damn it. Here, without thinking about it, I was riveted, aware of nothing more in this moment than that creature breathing in and out across from me.

For the first time, I was forced to think about strays. True to his kitten kind, Number Three was programmed from the paw up to be reach-out-your-arms-want-to-squeeze-him adorable. It wasn't his cartoon-eyed cuteness that got me. It was his curiosity. He had no fear at all, just pure interest. We've all had a late-night pas de deux with urban wildlife, the wild-eyed opossum or raccoon caught out in the open, the dash (or in the case of the opossum, the slow lollop) to safety behind a nearby trash can. Being with a creature I'd thought of as nothing but wild had jolted me. I couldn't get his gaze out of my mind.

I scanned the empty yard. The space still looked like what I expected of Union City, its pile of abandoned tiles, two car tires stacked on top of each other, an unchanging mess. Yet, it wasn't the same anymore. There were tiny beings in that yard that demanded a sense of the here and now. I knew there was only a sliver of time before that kitten would lose the ability to look a human in the face, his feral nature permanently imprinted on his identity. We either acted now, or he and his siblings would become wild, lost for good.

I swung my head back toward Matt. He looked so normal, oblivious to what was about to hit him.

"Matt," I said, walking into the kitchen, "we have to save the kittens."

To his credit, he kept smiling. Or maybe he just had no clue what I was saying.

"We can't let the kittens stay out there," I clarified in what I thought was a helpful tone.

"Okay," he replied. Did I mention Matt's not a big talker?

He tends to be quiet, but that doesn't mean he isn't paying attention. Just the opposite. Matt is observant. He hates disagreements and disappointing people. He was searching for the right answer.

He looked at me. I looked at him.

"We don't know anything about taking care of wild kittens," he managed to throw out as a stalling tactic.

"That's a good point," I conceded. He appeared so relieved that I felt bad adding, "What we need is some help."

Matt stared at me. I wasn't sure if it was the *we* in the phrase or the fact that I was still talking about this that confused him.

"We need to call someone," I explained.

"For the kittens?"

"Yeah. We need some advice."

"About how to rescue kittens?" he repeated, just to clarify that I wasn't speaking in tongues.

I nodded.

He paused, looking wistfully at the pile of cooling pancakes sitting on the table underneath a clear glass plate. Kittens out back had seemed like an amusing distraction, something to talk about over breakfast before moving on with the rest of the day. Matt had not planned for this.

"Maybe they're better off outside?" he asked.

He had a point. This could be true. I didn't know if strays weren't better off on their own outside. I had never considered it before. There had to be a reason why wild cats were out there, why you saw them but didn't think about them. Why when a friendly cat walked along the street, seeming lost, you felt obliged

15

to ask people walking by you whether they knew someone whose pet had escaped. But wild cats? What could you do about them? Maybe the fact that they seemed to be everywhere meant there was a reason they were outside.

Yet, at some point between the time that the kitten's tail disappeared through the tufts of weeds and my walk across the yard back to the house, a feeling took hold I couldn't shake. Three kittens outside wasn't right. Because we could do something about it, Matt and me.

I felt called upon, which was not like me. Giving back, getting outside myself, volunteering. I'd tried it all. I'd trekked up to Washington Heights to try to herd a bunch of eight-year-olds into their seats Saturday mornings so they would study. Spent afternoons in an overheated, dusty office on the East Side, attempting to help a local food co-op write the history of its organization. Nothing had stuck. Or rather, I didn't. I'd spend so much time trying to figure out what I was trying to accomplish (Change my view of the world? Make a difference? Break my brunch habit?) that before I knew it, I was back to waking at eleven on the weekends, unfettered and uncommitted.

The day was lovely. The kittens were fine outside. But I knew we needed to act. Matt didn't quite get it yet, okay. If Matt can embrace things on the spot when he feels they are right, why not me? I couldn't remember the last time I had done that.

"There is the Cat Practice," said Matt, interrupting my thoughts.

Of course there was. This was New York. Where else would you find the first vet in the United States started to cater exclusively to cats? I would soon learn that the Cat Practice was the New York headquarters for people who believed cats just made room for humans on earth. The office in the Flatiron District was run by Skip Sullivan, a six-foot ex-marine. Dr. Sullivan comfortably hung his Vietnam War bronze medal alongside a specially printed sign that read, "Our vets are fluent in Felinese and unabashedly pro-cat."

"I started going there when I adopted Teevee and Radio," Matt explained in his slow way. "Radio was sick, something he caught at the ASPCA. Now, Dr. Sullivan, he knows cats. There was this thing he would do, putting his mouth over Radio's nose to check his breathing."

He leaned over to demonstrate on Radio, who was sitting on the kitchen table. Radio jumped back in disgust.

"Huh," I said, because what else could you say? Matt was good at surprising me, often with detailed explanations about how condensation or pulley systems work. He made the generous assumption that I was following what he was saying, which I loved because it was so misplaced.

"The Cat Practice sounds perfect," I said, picking up the phone.

I described the situation to Yolanda, the receptionist who answered on the first ring. She didn't even bother handing me over to the vet after I explained what the kittens looked like, how they still stumbled around a little. From my description she decided they must be around four or five weeks old. Therefore, she was adamant.

"They can't be taken away from their mother before eight

weeks, Miss Green." Everyone at the Cat Practice called clients by their last name. It was very New York, 1950s.

"But they're outside, anything could happen to them."

"The mother's milk is the best thing for them right now," she replied in a Bronx accent, with its nasally As and Os and no-messing-around consonants. "They need to stay with her, darling." I later learned that Yolanda called everyone darling in a calm way, even suppliers she was berating for being late with medical deliveries. "Get them later, in a few weeks. Right now, you should feed the mother. That will help them more than anything else."

I held the phone against my cheek, brooding. Yolanda didn't hang up, even when I broke the silent treatment with a deep sigh.

In the amused voice of someone who was born and raised in New York and had heard it all, she said, "Trust me."

I calculated. Three, possibly four weeks of paranoia and torture. I thanked her before putting down the phone, knowing somehow, though I couldn't tell where this insight came from, that when it came to lining up help for the kittens, I needed to keep Yolanda on my good side.

"We have to wait," I said, turning to Matt, hoping to pull him along with my fake certainty about the path before us but not so sure he'd come along.

Matt assessed me. He could choose to battle it out. There were real stakes at play. If the kittens wound up in our hands, they were going to call Chez Matt home. There was no way we were going to transfer three wild animals via bus and subway to my apartment on the Upper West Side. Observant, considering Matt proved he got me more than I could explain myself in that moment.

He walked to the kitchen. I watched, elated, as he took a blue plastic dish out of the closet, put some cat food on it, and took it outside, not realizing what we were getting into. Not understanding that, through the summer adventure that followed of catching, taming, and finding homes for those little beings, we would be entering a strange new culture, one with its own rules, taboos, and characters.

Because how much harm could there be in feeding a few kittens?

2

Avoiding the Embroidery
Capital of the World

Cat rescuer. That's the very last badge I ever expected to wear. Did I mention I'm allergic to the little menaces? Until the kittens came along, I was trying my best to avoid spending too much time in Union City, New Jersey, where Matt and his cats—and now a few more strays—lived.

I met Matt when I was happily settling into being single. We ran into each other at a backyard party in Harlem in May 2004. We'd socialized in the same crowd for years, getting together at parties, movies, and restaurants where we'd apparently met many times. I say apparently, because until that day, if someone had said, "Hey, look, there's Matt over by the drinks table," I wouldn't have known if they meant the tall guy with the crazy brown hair sticking out in all directions or the dog wagging its tail next to him. Well, that's an exaggeration. I knew the dog's name was Otto.

Our streak was set to continue that day. When Matt arrived at the party and came outside and sat next to me in the garden, I was too busy chatting with the woman across the table to pay attention to him. I love parties because I like hearing people's stories, where they came from, what makes them tick. It's the reporter in me. Matt says this is my superpower, this ability I have to get people to talk. New York is full of folks with stories, starting with what compelled them to brave this frantic, loud, competitive city. Later that afternoon, I flitted from one conversation to the next, not paying attention to anyone in particular, not picking up on the fact that Matt was taking me in.

Valentine, a matchmaking older Jamaican gentleman at the party, noticed. He observed how Matt watched me, saw him go inside to refill my glass with the same red wine I'd been drinking. Matt told me later that he hadn't been sure, earlier in the day, that he wanted to make the trek from downtown Manhattan up to Harlem. He'd been lying in a hammock in the backyard of the apartment he rented, loafing away the morning. But sitting beside me in the early-afternoon breeze at the party, he'd noticed me for the first time and was glad he'd made the trip. The problem was, in the face of all my excited chattering, he didn't have much of a chance of getting *me* to notice *him*.

He didn't need to worry. Valentine was on the case. As the afternoon get-together wound down, our hosts Erik and Gail announced that they planned to go to the movies a couple of blocks away on 125th Street. Did anyone else want to go along?

That's when Valentine took me and Matt in hand. As our small group made its way through the theater lobby, Valentine looped his arm through mine. Then he reached around behind and tugged Matt forward.

"You two sit together," he laughed, pushing us in front of him through the doors of the theater and walking down the aisle after us to make sure we followed his directions. "No sense wasting a nice, dark movie theater on an old man like me," he said, nodding his gray head when we sat down next to each other. Mission accomplished, Valentine shuffled back up the aisle to get some popcorn and gossip with some of his neighborhood friends in the lobby.

I laughed, self-conscious. How often do you get paired up so obviously? I looked at Matt, really taking him in for the first time and realizing upon inspection that I was happy to be sitting in the dark with this fellow. Matt was attractive, in the tall, lean, brown-haired way I like. He had a wide mouth and an easy way of holding his shoulders. Settled, relaxed. As the trailers started rolling, we both slunk down in our seats, our shoulders touching, warm. We laughed at the same points during the epically bad trailer for *Garfield: The Movie*. As the notes of "Wild Thing" faded away along with the image of an animated boogying cat, Matt said in a deadpan voice, "We should definitely see that." I laughed. I always do when he tosses out that same short phrase, summing up something we definitely shouldn't do. Like how he later would say, "We should open a restaurant that puts truffle oil on everything," as we passed by La Tartufferia, a short-lived place in Hoboken we went to that turned us both off that ingredient.

Walking slowly to the subway later in the dark with Matt, I recall brushing up against his arm a couple of times and explaining with an uncharacteristically breathy laugh that this habit of walking into people is a trait my family shares. We're a group of weavers, though we only ever bump into people we like.

Matt and I waited in an awkward silence on the platform, checking each other out once again under the bright focus of fluorescent lights. A train came into the station, and a few Yankees fans, returning from a night game, got off at our stop.

Matt cleared his throat. "I'm going to a game next week. The Yankees, I mean," he said. "They're struggling this year again with their pitching staff." His voice trailed off.

I looked at him. It was a humid evening, and he was sweating through the front of his light blue shirt. I later learned that he sweats a lot. He was self-conscious about it, which I found endearing.

I considered Matt, liking his kind eagerness. He was interested, and that was flattering. But also irritating.

At thirty-six, I was finally, happily single. This is a state that is not to be underestimated. I'd seen it all. The reliable guys whose willingness to commit bored or scared me. The delinquents I stuck with who knows why. The bolters, sometimes me and sometimes them. All those repetitive, ultimately boring internal monologues circling around the same questions: Why was I alone? When would I not be alone?

When I was living in Paris in my twenties, I had a French boyfriend who tried to persuade me not to go back to the United States because he knew the end result would be me lying on a therapist's couch talking about my mother. "Cela arrive à tous les Américains," Guillaume teased me, having seen all of Woody Allen's films along with the rest of his country. I didn't stay, and he was right in the end. Thank goodness. After many hours on a leather sofa (really) talking to my therapist, Susan, who was smart enough to know when I was lying and why, I moved into hard-won happiness. At a dinner with a partnered-up crowd, I could give a straight answer, without waggling quotation fingers, when asked what my dating status was. I stopped trying to borrow my friends' husbands when I was invited to evenings at the suburban homes of older work colleagues and their wives. Happily single at last.

So now, out of nowhere, this guy? This heart-thumping, head-buzzing attraction?

It was annoying.

I knew a grand total of three things about Yankees baseball: (1) Derek Jeter, the guy who was always on the cover of the *New York Post* because of his disco escapades at the time, played for them; (2) People did play polo back in the day at the Polo Grounds, a stadium in Manhattan the Yankees briefly called home; (3) Saying the Yankees' pitching staff was bad was like saying it was raining in Seattle. It was nearly always true.

Beyond these bits of data, I was lost. As a journalist, I was good at fudging knowledge just enough to get other people to talk. Another express train went by. Matt shoved his hands deeper into his pockets. Teetering between interest and irritation, I decided to give in but just barely.

"I think I read about that. Remind me who is pitching for them this year?" I asked.

Matt was off, obviously relieved he'd hit on a subject that would keep us talking for the next ten minutes until we stepped on the subway. By the time the train lurched to a halt at my stop at 72nd Street, I knew a great deal about the Yankees' pitching starters, relievers, and trades. I also knew that Matt was an earnest, funny nerd. I found it charming when he revealed that he was an old-school baseball fan who marked up scorecards. I appreciated how he asked questions about my sixteen-year-old nephew, Marley, when I mentioned that the kid managed to live down south and like the Yankees. I was, despite my hesitation about jumping back into the whirlwind of attraction, curious about this fellow sitting next to me on the orange subway bench. I was nervous, giddy. It was fun. I wanted to interest this fellow because he interested me. I thought I was doing a pretty good job, even if my flirting skills were a little rusty. As I stood up to make my exit, lingering by the open doorway, I expected him to ask for my phone number. But he let me go. I walked home, disappointed, bereft, certain that I had let my conflicting emotions show as if they'd been little bubbles floating over my head, kicking myself for not just taking more of a risk and getting his number first.

That Monday at work, an email from Matt popped into my box. He wanted to invite me and Erik and Gail, our mutual friends who had held the party, to the baseball game. I was ecstatic. I felt noticed, special to someone who seemed unique to me. I liked this ripple of nerve-jangling feelings.

I later learned that just as the subway doors closed after me,

Matt realized he'd been so caught up in our conversation that he'd forgotten to get my phone number. He spent the next few seconds kicking himself because he was sure he'd never find me again in New York City.

But then it dawned on him, of course. He could ask Erik, at whose parties we had met so many times over the past decade.

I felt lucky to have met Matt. New Jersey, where he lived, I wasn't so sure about.

I'd moved fifteen times in my life before settling down in Manhattan to cover Internet-related stories for *BusinessWeek* when I was thirty. With an Air Force pilot as a father, I became an expert at change, at getting up and going when I grew bored or uncomfortable. A little too expert. All through college and into my late twenties, I never stayed put. I traveled around Europe, returned to the United States for college, lived in France for a few years, and then headed home. I'd accumulated a lot of experiences to blend into a sense of who I was, but I never managed to do just that. Instead, I'd become adept at losing touch with friends and collecting many ex-boyfriends. I had avoided the hard work of settling into the world around me.

In 2001, *BusinessWeek* offered to move me to Silicon Valley from New York to cover the startups that had come to define that area. For a tech writer, that was like achieving nirvana. Yet, if the opportunity was so great, why wasn't I excited?

This new job offer presented me with a choice. Either I kept waltzing around and became an ever more flittering shadow or I could try staying put and start filling in those hazy contours.

I opted to make a go at setting down roots. I turned down the job. I needed to stop and see what it was like to sit tight for once. In Manhattan.

I know. Crazy.

New York is the shallowest plot of dirt on earth. Everyone is busy, all the time. You have to work hard, push at building friendships, at staying connected, at climbing up the ladder. But it was my bit of ground. I was here and I was staying. I had found some promising new friends, good work colleagues, and, necessary for a basic level of sanity in New York City, a psychotherapist I couldn't bullshit.

I made plans to run (badly) the New York City Marathon with my friend Brigid. I found a new apartment on the Upper West Side, a block away from Central Park, that was big enough for more than just two people to stand up in, and I had guests over. I walked everywhere, torn by the inevitable, energetic renewal of Manhattan's lonely waterfronts and grimy pockets, memorizing Greenwich Village's twisting streets by sheer repetition, and proud of my ability to avoid horse manure on the Central Park bridle path before the last stable in Manhattan closed and that talent became obsolete.

The process of making a home in Manhattan that I was going through was basic but, for the first time, deliberate.

Then I met Matt and, after two years of being together, I

could add sticking with a boyfriend to my list of accomplishments.

Now . . . after settling into the idea of being a New Yorker, I was being confronted with New Jersey. I liked my shiny competitive city, with its familiar bustle and expectation of who fits in where and what you want out of life.

A former textile hub directly across the Hudson River from Manhattan, Union City did not buzz. Union City was where arrivals from Central and South America lived the dream of today's first-generation immigrants, working seventy-hour weeks as nannies, bus drivers, and dishwashers. Mayor Brian P. Stack (the P. was in every printed mention of his name—the plaques on parks around town, the city mailings, the sides of the city trucks) helpfully sent out fliers advertising meetings for gang-awareness training and free Thanksgiving turkeys. If you needed a money order service for sending cash out of the country, you were in luck. They lined Bergenline Avenue, the town's main shopping street.

Almost everyone going into New York speeds past Union City without knowing it, zipping under a sign, a bit of bygone glory that announces, "Welcome to North New Jersey, Embroidery Capital of the World Since 1872." That is this particular community's fate, to always be the kind of place most people pass through. Really fast.

The truth is, there isn't much of a reason to pause. Union City is a no-nonsense working-class neighborhood with vinyl-clad row houses locked up behind chain-link fences and weeds colonizing the cracks in the sidewalks. The first time I took the bus from Port Authority bus terminal in New York to spend the weekend with Matt, the only sign of life I saw was a few people sitting in plastic chairs in front of their houses. Even the trees lining the road, their leaves dusty, looked inert. This place was heads down, on the edge, though not giving an inch.

I got why Matt liked the house he'd bought. It was a compact two-story redbrick row house with a lot of light, an amenity that's mythical in most New York apartments. As a bonus, it had a series of second-story windows where, every once in a while, if you craned your head just right, you could spot the Empire State Building through the trees. His street, Manhattan Avenue, was known as the nicest block in Union City. Though with a clear division. On the east side, on the edge of the Palisade cliffs that overlook the Hudson River and Manhattan, were substantial brick houses with front porches and back gardens owned by the Germans and Italians who first settled the town, many building embroidery factories that later attracted Cuban workers in the 1940s. On the west side of the street was Matt's home, huddled up close to a clutch of five other row houses belonging to Hispanic families.

Matt loved this community. Union City was a little bit desolate. It wasn't brash like New York. It was harder to pigeonhole people here. Matt, an observer, fit into this off-kilter place. I appreciated that Matt liked to be on the outside, that he was drawn to seemingly forgotten places and people. As someone who spent all day listening to very successful people on the phone talk about themselves in my work as a journalist, his ability to empathize with the tossed-off rather than the bright and sparkly is part of what drew me to him.

The summer we first started dating, I called Matt, excited about an upcoming program in Central Park.

"The parks department is offering a bat walk! We should go," I exclaimed. I'd loved bats ever since my father killed one when we first moved to the old farmhouse my parents bought in Virginia when I was twelve. Bats lived in the attic, and every once in a while one would flutter into the main part of the house late at night through the attic door left open by mistake. My father would run after the creature with a tennis racket as it swooped and flittered from room to room. Usually, he disposed of it before any of us could see it. But one morning, I saw the body next to the back porch. I moved forward, drawn to the wizened being. A broad, bloody tear stretched the length of the right wing. Maybe that's what did it in. Then the bat turned its face just a bit. I jumped back, startled by its sharp row of teeth, but also struck by how helpless its eyes looked. It was a smidge of a thing, more frightened of me than I could ever be of it. After that, especially when I learned that bats were champions at eating mosquitoes, I became a bat admirer.

"Bats?" Matt repeated.

"Yes, I love them! There is a group meeting up at eight thirty and going on a bat-sighting tour through Central Park."

"Central Park. At night?" Matt was part of the generation of New Yorkers taught never to go into Central Park after dark. Things had changed a lot over the past decade, but old habits about bodily security and avoiding being mugged die hard.

Still, Matt went along because I was so thrilled. Delayed by a slow subway, we turned up late at the meeting place on Central Park West to find that there wasn't a bat-sighting soul in sight. We tried to catch up with the group in the park, but we never spotted them or bats. Matt wasn't too disappointed. Secretly convinced that I'd been scheming to find a quiet place to make out, he took advantage of a spot under a London plane tree near the 72nd Street exit to kiss for a while. What I loved about the whole adventure was that he never thought it odd that I adored an animal that made most people duck and scream.

Matt was accepting. Yet, there was something about his stillness that bothered me, something reflected in his house. He had done a lot of work, plastering the walls and painting them. But, though he had moved in two years before, there were still boxes everywhere. He was a collector of things, a maker of piles. When Matt wants something, he disappears into the basement for a while and sifts through piles. Sometimes he even finds what he's looking for.

The most perplexing part to me was that none of this seemed to bother him. It made me wonder about him, about our differences. My one-bedroom apartment in Manhattan was organized down to the Aurora fountain pen my brother gave me for my birthday. Boxes, piles: that was chaos in my eyes. How committed could you be to your plans for your life if you couldn't find the basic stuff needed to build them?

During one weekend at Matt's house, I had tried unsuccessfully to track down a Sunday *New York Times* and taken in a remarkable variety of vinyl siding and an impressive number of auto-repair shops during my search. I had gazed at his piles of stuff. After that, I had managed to persuade Matt to spend most weekends at my place in Manhattan. I hadn't figured out what it meant for our relationship. I avoided thinking about that. All I knew was that I wanted roots, just maybe not here, on these terms. It was a state of affairs that had lasted for about eighteen months.

Then the trio of kittens showed up.

The Monday morning after we found the litter, I got to my desk in Midtown on my way to a brighter outlook thanks to a small coffee, light and sweet, from the Pakistani food cart guy in front of my building. I was armed with a plan for the cats. Between the calls that I had set up for a feature I was writing about new developments in wireless technology, I was going to scour the Internet until I mastered everything there was to know about rescuing cats.

And then I promptly dropped the ball. Back in office mode, with emails to answer, calls to set up, photos to assign, the kittens' plight lost its urgency and importance. My newfound sense of commitment to something outside myself was no match to my devotion to my profession. I was at the office all the time. One Saturday on the way to *BusinessWeek*'s office tower, I was so tired from the series of late nights my team had pulled that week that I walked smack into a red and white striped pole on the subway platform. I sat on the floor of the station for fifteen

minutes, hovered over by a tattooed and pierced twentysomething fellow who had witnessed the pole/head encounter. Despite the huge knot blossoming over my eye and the worried
protests of my impromptu nurse, I got up and hustled to my desk.
My colleagues prevailed, persuading me to take a taxi to the ER
at St. Vincent's Hospital. (Though notice none of them left their
computers to take me there. We all played by the same work
code.)

Complete dedication to my career was normal to me. When
I was first hired by *BusinessWeek* but before I started, I asked a
friend to help me lug some things to the office on a Sunday
afternoon. My boss, a first-class workaholic, greeted us as we
wandered down the corridor.

"I'm always here on Sundays if you need anything," she
chirped. "I just get so much done."

"Very bad sign," my friend Valerie mumbled.

I just looked at Valerie, trying to figure out what she meant.

The kittens, though, wouldn't be denied. What was surprising was who turned out to be the driving force behind their
rescue campaign.

On Tuesday morning, at my desk and digging through the
two hundred emails I had received overnight, I spotted a message from Matt. It was sent at 2 A.M. I clicked it open, and my
inbox sprang to life with a lineup of photos. Matt had had a busy
evening.

I had only seen one of the kittens clearly so far. But here they were in digital color. In his email, Matt explained he had named them Zero, Two Spot, and Number Three because of their markings. The first few pictures were of my little guy, Number Three. Matt had taken a shot of him behind the metal shed in the neighbor's backyard. The kitten was circling around an abandoned plastic bucket, jumping over it, sitting next to it. In the next group of photos, he was looking up at the camera and, true to form, stalking over toward the unfamiliar gadget. I could just imagine him seeing Matt or hearing something above his head and trotting nearer to investigate what had made the noise, not scared at all.

In the next shot, one of his siblings toddled up beside him. This second kitten, Zero, was smaller, more delicate, almost all white except for a negligible splotch of black on his head next to his right ear and an all-black tail. In the next image, I got my first glimpse of all three of them together. The third kitten, Two Spot, had enormous ears. I gazed at them for a minute and figured out that they looked massive because his face was blindingly white while his ears were dark tabby brown. He was like a Japanese anime character. Two Spot was lankier. Or as lanky as a tubby, fuzzy kitten could be. No bigger than my hand, these kittens were miracles of survival.

I was mesmerized. I expected to feel responsibility. I'm dependable. I send out thank-you notes promptly. I'm so good at paying my bills on time that once, when I called American Express customer service about some charge on my bill, the guy at the call center complimented me on my timely payments. I could tell he meant it. But this was more than a feeling of responsibility. I looked at a picture of the three of them contemplating Matt and his camera, eager to take a swipe out of curiosity. I wanted to see them. I was happy knowing they were around, three bumbling little bodies discovering the world. Then the phone rang. It was the receptionist. My 9:30 A.M. meeting was waiting in the lobby. I grabbed my notebook and pen. Back to work.

The next day, Matt reported that he had devised a way to play with them over the fence with a supersized fishing pole of his own devising: attaching a long piece of string to the end of a mop pole for them to chase. The kittens loved playing, especially Two Spot and Number Three.

Now I was getting worried. We had agreed, or I thought we had, that we would just feed them so that they became acclimated to people. Matt, the person who had chosen a neighborhood devoid of coffee shops and corner stores stocked with organic milk so he could avoid trendy crowds, liked hanging out with the kittens.

"Be careful about not scaring them off by watching them too much. Mother cats get protective and will move them," I wrote in a return email, invoking all the country childhood knowledge I had about cats.

Later in the day another email showed up, one that revealed just how seriously Matt was taking this. The message contained a link to a Web site. Underneath he wrote: "Here's a workshop that I found on the ASPCA's site for catching feral cats. The group looks kind of crazy and it's twenty-five dollars and I don't know how they use that money. But I signed up for it." Matt had started his own fact-finding while I had been ignoring my own cat-rescuing research, I realized with a guilty feeling.

When I called Matt that night, I joked that he was becoming a crazy cat person.

"I like the kittens, but I'm doing this for you," he protested without a pause.

"You're playing with them every night because of me?" I teased.

"Well, not only because of you," he admitted. "Two Spot loves the fishing pole I made and is he ever a jumper. Oh, and the most amazing thing I wanted to tell you. I'm starting to see the mother. She's eating with the kittens."

The mother? I couldn't believe I had missed out on the first sighting of her. She was beautiful, he explained, all white, with a black tail and a smidge of black on her head. He had named her Oona.

"After all," he explained, "she's number one." Then without warning, he added, "Heather, I'm still not sure this is the right move. Catching them, I mean."

I listened, not wanting to interrupt. When Matt does or says something he thinks might upset you, he does it slowly. He's also good at putting on bandages and removing splinters.

"Seeing her with them, you know how happy they are together," he explained. "They're a family. Breaking them up could go wrong. We don't know what we're doing."

I hadn't seen what Matt had, Oona and her boys together. Seeing them together would definitely make it harder to consider splitting them up. But I had been doing my own reading, and the arguments the rescue folks made for bringing the kittens inside and finding homes for them were that it was better for the whole family, even if it might be awful for them at first. I knew too well how easy it was to just decide not to do something because it was unfamiliar. I'd done that plenty of times. Matt wasn't like me. He takes on the unknown once he believes in something. Bringing these concerns up showed how much thought he was giving the project.

"Matt, you know that advice you give me whenever I'm uncertain about how things will turn out? You tell me to take things one step at a time, that I can adjust along the way. You know how hard that is for me," I laughed in a low tone. "Let's try that now."

Matt was quiet.

"Oona is gorgeous," he finally said. "The way her muscles flow under her white coat. Beautiful. She's getting used to me," he added, his voice easing. "Instead of running at me to try to scare me away when I put down the food, she only hisses."

"She runs at you?"

"Not anymore. You'll see."

I did. That Friday night I got on the 123 bus to Union City, exhausted after a jam-packed workweek. The bus rattled around the helix, the massive curved ramp that takes you out of the Lincoln Tunnel and up onto the Palisades, the cliffs of New Jersey overlooking the Hudson River. The view of the

Manhattan skyline from the helix at the end of the day was breathtaking. All the disappointment and success, the buckets of money lost and made, the egos inflated and destroyed, the time spent on therapists' couches or in bars, all that energy was compressed together, creating the line of towering buildings glowing in the sunset.

At the top of the ramp, just as a band of trees on the cliffs blocked the view of Manhattan, the bus turned off Route 495 at a sign marked "Weehawken, Union City." For the first time, I was excited to see those words, eager to spend time with the kittens after being away from them for an entire week.

I jumped off the bus at Matt's stop, sprinting across the hot boulevard, past the tidy, red slate–roofed stone church on the corner, and took a right turn on Manhattan Avenue. Rushing through Matt's front door, I made straight for the back of the house where I could see my boyfriend standing on the back porch.

He stepped inside, greeting me with a long, warm kiss.

"Welcome back," he said, smiling that sharp curved smile of his that was so wide and relaxed.

It felt like coming home, with five beings—a family of cats and a man—waiting for me.

Matt hadn't given them their dinner yet. He'd waited for me to witness the excitement. As he opened the cans of kitten food, I peeked over the edge of the concrete wall, disappointed to see that the lot was empty.

"They aren't there, Matt," I reported to him, worried.

"You don't think they are, but you'll see," he laughed. "They're growing boys. They never miss a meal."

He walked out to join me, stepping down to creak open the gate between the two adjoining backyards. He moved forward, placing the blue plastic plate with a careful gesture on the ground. Then, just as deliberately, he retreated, coming to stand next to me. It was quiet back here. I could hear the English ivy leaves rippling in the breeze, the sound of a child's laughter through the windows of the church daycare—and then a faint sound of crunching paper coming from behind the metal shed that slumped in the back corner of Roberto's lot.

A white head emerged on stealthy paws from the weeds that lined the shed. Oona stepped forward. Oona was a glamorous cat, long, lanky, and graceful. I was stunned at how beautiful she was. Gazing around with the cool, deliberate look of a lioness, she checked for other cats, other threats. Reassured, Oona proceeded, unhurried and sure, toward the plate. The next moment, complete pandemonium broke the spell. The three kittens tumbled through the tall grass, sprinting toward the plate in a jumble of legs and tails. They were all so low to the ground and bunched up it was hard to tell where one kitten ended and another began. Careening forward in a furry bunch, they crashed into their elegant mother, who managed to remain standing and unflustered by the pile of black-and-white kittens at her feet. With three quick heaves, they jumped up onto their paws, lowered their heads, and began gobbling away.

I couldn't take my eyes off them. They were more diminutive

than I remembered. But they were just as adorable as the photos I had gazed at all week. When it came to eating, I saw that Matt was right. They were intense, concentrated. Playing and growing took a lot of energy. They gulped and licked until the blue plate was clean. Exhausted by so much eating, the kittens toddled over to an abandoned wooden door lying on the ground and collapsed. Oona followed, sitting next to them and pulling each one forward with her paws to lick their faces and ears until all four dropped off asleep, curled together.

Our cats.

That weekend, we discovered that Matt's little stretch of Union City was feline central. On a trip to the deli down the block the next day, I spotted three different strays in the bushes, on a stoop, darting down an alleyway. On a walk down to Hoboken for dinner, we saw a white and orange feline slinking through a small parking lot down the street. We even saw Oona across the street, spending time with one male in particular that Matt decided to call Owen.

These weren't house cats slipping out the kitchen window for a slow wander around the block. They were wild. These strays were programmed to avoid people. They crept along, their bodies low to the ground. They stayed close to cars and trash cans so that they could duck under them at the first sign of a human. Their existence depended on sizing up every situation every minute, on living on their guard.

Sunday evening, leaning against the outside brick wall of Matt's house, watching the kittens, I realized that all the neighborhood's outside cats started out like Two Spot, Number Three, and Zero. They might have been born under a stoop somewhere, but that didn't mean they were destined to be wary or alone. Our boys were carefree and secure under the gaze of a vigilant mother. I watched as they sprinted across the concrete. Two Spot jumped straight up in the air for no apparent reason other than that he could. Number Three sputtered to a halt just as Two Spot hit the ground, dropped down low on his paws, and then jumped sideways at Number Three. Zero, who never played as rough as the other two, waited until his brothers were distracted and rolling around in a ball of black-and-white limbs. Seizing his chance, he leapt on top of them.

Oona observed their antics from her favorite perch on top of the concrete fence on the far side of the yard. She stood up, stretching her long white legs in a languid way that reminded me of a 1930s starlet, before settling down again.

Below, on the concrete patio, Zero, Two Spot, and Number Three were lying on top of one another. Number Three alternated between batting Zero's twitching tail and thumping Two Spot's head. A brick dug into my shoulder, and I moved slightly. Attuned to any change around them, the kittens looked up. Recognizing me, they rolled over again instead of running and hiding under the pile of doors. I had my doubts about Union City, about Matt and me, even about whether I was capable of the responsibility these kittens entailed. But watching them right now, I realized I wanted more than anything to try.

3

Tiptoeing into the Fray

Our first order of business was getting a trap. Matt had gone through the training with Neighborhood Cats, the cat rescue group in Manhattan, because if anyone was going to deal with the trap's fast-closing metal gate, it was him, not me. Neighborhood Cats did lend out cages, they just wouldn't let them cross the Hudson River. They will instruct New Jerseyites, but they won't arm them. We tried to track down traps to buy, but after calling three Home Depots and a few local hardware stores, we realized that no one had the extra-special cat cage that we needed.

Of course, no ordinary device would do. Raccoons, opossums, any old trap works for them. We're talking cats, though. Feral or not, they demand more. In this case, a roomy cage with two doors. When it comes to a raccoon, the whole goal is catch and release. Catching feral cats, that is an entirely different proposition.

Because what Matt had learned when he attended the Neighborhood Cats workshop was that we needed to do more than just catch the kittens and find homes for them. To get at the real problem—Oona having kittens outside in the first place—we needed to trap her, too, get her fixed, and put her back outside. Unlike the kittens, she was too wild to bring in. So the best we could do for her and the community was to make sure she didn't have any more kittens. Essentially, we would practice on a small scale an approach called TNR, or Trap-Neuter-Return, that began gaining ground among rescue groups in the 1990s as a way to reduce the number of strays and give cats outside a healthier life.

So we needed a trap for catching the kittens. But fixing a cat, as we were now determined to do with Oona after we caught the kittens, is all about catch and keep. That requires a specially designed trap. Between the initial catch, the operation itself, and recovering from her surgery, Oona would have to stay in the cage for a few days. Cat traps are longer than regular animal traps and have two doors, one on either side, so you can feed the often perturbed furry occupant and change the paper inside the cage more easily.

We'd hit a wall. Then Matt—a man who will do everything possible to avoid telephoning someone he doesn't know—picked up the phone and called Tomahawk, the family-owned business in Wisconsin that makes the extra-special cages. They were temporarily out of stock, he was told on the phone. But, in the loony world of rescuing, that stumbling block didn't matter one bit. Without hesitating, the woman on the other end of the line gave Matt the number of Joan, a local cat rescuer in the neighboring town of Weehawken who bought a lot of traps from the company. Call her and ask to borrow one, she told him.

Naturally, Matt phoned me.

"Can you contact Joan?" Matt asked.

"She gave you Joan's number?" I repeated, bewildered and also impressed not just that the secretary had made the suggestion, but that Matt had called the company.

"Yeah, without me even asking. Oh, and she also gave me Joan's address. I Googled her. She lives just ten minutes away from my house."

"The company that sells cages is telling you to borrow one?" I asked. This did not strike me as a sound business practice.

"She said that she knows cat people can't wait. Somehow she knows that this Joan person lends traps out all the time."

"Who are these people we're getting involved with?"

"Exactly," he agreed. There was a happy sense of connection over the phone. Then he repeated, "Can you call Joan?"

"You just phoned the cat cage company. What's the difference with calling Joan?" I asked, perplexed.

"I'm used to dealing with companies, not people," Matt said.

I waited for him to say more. After a few seconds of silence, I realized that that was it. That was Matt's explanation. Employees at a company weren't regular humans, so they didn't break his code of not talking to too many people. I agreed to call Joan.

I'd later learn that Joan, in her mid-fifties, was short and sturdy with cropped gray hair and crooked teeth protruding out of a wise mouth. Compact and rough-hewn, she looked like a coal stoker. Joan, though, had the mind of a great Cold War diplomat. I could easily imagine her exchanging prisoners on snow-covered bridges in Eastern Europe in the 1950s. Joan was scientific, systematic, and strategic in her approach to all things cat rescue. At an adoption event or meeting, in her usual gray sweatshirt, you'd never notice her. But she was there, I'd soon learn, working in the background, chatting up folks, cultivating connections.

Joan was not born a cat person. A sleight of paw ushered her into the feline orbit. On a fall day about twenty years before I met her, a stray showed up, nosing around for food in her backyard as if he'd gotten an invitation to dinner. Joan soon found herself regularly feeding the fellow, who knew it paid to be a courteous gentleman. She dubbed him Grayson but didn't give him much thought beyond this daily ritual.

One day, as he sauntered across the road to her house, she watched him get clipped by a car. Urbane as ever, Grayson bounced up off the pavement and trotted over, as if to apologize for worrying her. More shaken than Grayson, Joan rushed him inside and closed him in the bedroom for a while. Half an hour later, she turned around in the kitchen, and there was the cat, sitting on the table, watching her politely. Joan picked him up and put him back in the bedroom. Ten minutes later, Grayson wandered in again. This time, Joan sat in the bedroom with him. Grayson meandered around a bit and then, sure that life was more interesting outside, ambled toward the door where her handbag hung on the doorknob. Reaching up with a casual paw, he pulled the bag, which turned the handle and opened the door. Glancing back at her with a come-along-now look, Grayson wandered off to explore. That was that. Joan adopted her first cat.

What came next turned her into a rescuer: Grayson had FIV, or feline AIDS. Twenty years ago, this was a death sentence. Instead, Joan went to Whiskers Holistic Pet Care on Manhattan's Lower East Side, an earnest place—with glass jars stuffed with herbs lining the shelves—that specializes in homeopathic remedies.

"I need some help dealing with an FIV cat," she said to the manager.

Heads swiveled in the store.

"FIV? My cat has that, too," four or five other customers chimed in. Joan had found her people. And her people recommended a high-vitamin diet. Grayson, who Joan initially expected to die within two or three years, lived until he was seventeen.

After that, Joan was all cats all the time. The second stray that showed up in her yard (and there is always a second) had feline leukemia, or FeLV. Joan's house seemed to be a hot zone of killer diseases. Instead of panicking, she researched, and she eventually started an online FeLV group to share information. To help move adoptions along, she opened a pet store she ran for nine years, finding homes for thousands of cats. As a result of a New Jersey Commission investigation that exposed the deplorable conditions at the local humane society, she helped start a new shelter. You've heard of doers. Joan is one of those.

When we got in touch with her, Joan had returned to what first got her involved with cat rescuing: finding homes for difficult-to-love felines, the ones with diabetes, FIV, and other health issues.

Joan didn't miss a beat when I called and introduced myself, explaining that she didn't know me, but that a lady (I didn't know her name) at the cat cage manufacturer (I couldn't remember its name) suggested we call and borrow a trap.

"That's great!" Joan enthused. Her voice was low and a bit gruff, and she talked in nonstop run-on sentences that were hard to follow at first. "Three kittens and a mother? Wonderful. Don't do kittens anymore. Lost too many. But good for you!"

Lost? Sure, they're small, but how do you lose them . . . unless she meant in the permanent sense. I was on the verge of asking for clarification when I decided that I didn't want to know.

Joan was oblivious to my silence. She kept tripping along without a stop, so when I tuned back in, I found that she was explaining that her house was the little blue Victorian, that she wouldn't be home the evening we wanted to pick up the cage, but she was happy to leave the trap out on her front porch for us.

"Oh," she added, packing words together even more tightly. "Can you make sure to get it back soon? There's this couple. Haven't met them, either. They're in Jersey City and have a group of cats they're feeding behind their home. They want to borrow all of my cages."

"No problem. So, um, Joan, how many traps do you have anyway?"

"Well," she said, pausing for the first time. The silence was so abrupt and unexpected that I wondered if I had overstepped. Was it an unstated taboo in the cat community to ask how many felines or traps a person had?

"Four," she drawled. She had just been totaling up a mental list in her head. "Glad you asked. I've been lending them out so much lately I'm not sure where they all are. Things get crazy during kitten season." She paused for a split second, thrust back into thought again. "Though it's not yet like Florida where they have litters all year. But March to November, that's pretty close, right?"

Kitten . . . season? There's enough of them born to name an entire time period after them? We were in deeper than we thought. With all the cats around us, we must be surrounded by litters. We just hadn't spotted them yet.

"Though not as many make it up here because of the cold weather," Joan mused in a quiet tone, before adding, "As people get the hang of catching cats, they get faster at returning the traps. So as you and that other couple get better at this, I won't have to worry about the equipment." It took me a minute to realize she was talking about us.

"Joan," I managed to break in, though I couldn't figure out how to phrase how wrong she was. Joan was being generous, but the last thing I wanted to know was how, based on her extensive experience with the evolution of novice cat people, Matt and I would develop as future rescuers. Just the idea that we might get so much practice that we would get good at using the traps made me want to throw away Joan's number right after I said good-bye.

What I knew, despite Joan's predictions, was that I didn't have time to devote to becoming a crazy cat person. I was a driven New Yorker. For the first time, I was in charge of the magazine's annual list of the top one hundred tech companies in the world. A big responsibility full of career-making or career-destroying possibilities. *BusinessWeek*'s editors were mad for ranking things: business schools, golf courses, philanthropists, you name it, we put a number next to it and lined it up in a row. Lists give you a lot to do. Beyond managing a string of deadlines over the next month for the project, I also had to corral our Asian and European reporters into helping, which was a lot like herding cats since this group of oddball writers become foreign correspondents, far from the reach of editors, just to avoid being managed.

At the same time, scheduling the dinners and brunches necessary to keep up with my career-minded girlfriends, not to mention factoring in the cancellations and postponements caused by business trips, dates, and hangovers, was like arranging high-level diplomatic negotiations. Throwing cat trapping and its own particular sense of feline timing into the mix was insanity. We were just visiting the rescuing world. Sort of a pop-in stay.

Two nights after my first phone call with Joan, we were the proud borrowers of a certified cat-capturing trap, lent to us by a woman who'd never met us, arranged through someone at a company that was supposed to sell these things. It all made sense, in the feline scheme of things.

Having the cage, which we tucked away in the basement,

was a revelation. It made me feel like the candy man in *Chitty Chitty Bang Bang*, the dancing, skipping fellow who trapped all the children with clever trickery. Though I would use my powers for good, not evil.

There was something pretty heady about having a trap.

Spending time with the kittens on the weekends was eye-opening. We became avid cat watchers, following every move the litter made. Number Three, Two Spot, and Zero liked to eat and always sprinted forward whenever Oona showed up from her rounds to nurse them or when Matt put out the blue plate we'd dedicated to them. They were even more thrilled, though, by their growing bodies. They were gaining more control over their galloping limbs so that they didn't simply lollop around and trip over their legs every few feet. Instead, they were becoming miniature Chinese acrobats, tumbling and jumping over one another. One Saturday morning, as I stood on the edge of Matt's deck, following their antics over the fence, I watched as Two Spot, nosing around in some grass, spotted a butterfly fluttering above him. He started wandering after it, head tilting from side to side as he tried to figure out what it was, unaware of anything except this fascinating flying thing. Number Three, lying on his side on the ground, rolled with slow deliberation to his feet and began stalking his brother from behind through the grass. When the butterfly alighted on a long piece of grass, Two Spot sat back on his haunches to observe it. Creeping up behind, Number Three halted. He crouched down behind his brother, back end swaying side to side in preparation, and launched himself on Two Spot, who landed with a thump, his eyes wide and startled until he realized how he'd ended up on the ground. Wheeling around, he started batting Number Three on his head. It was a losing battle until Zero, ever careful to time his forays into the fray, jumped in and attacked Number Three, too. Outnumbered, Number Three leapt up and sprinted away, casting a triumphant look behind at his two siblings tumbling in the dirt.

Matt's giant fishing pole made out of a mop was also a huge hit. He had become an expert at manipulating it over the side of the fence. Number Three and Two Spot always noticed the string as soon as it appeared. They jumped and lunged at the line as Matt wiggled it along the ground. Two Spot was especially good at tracking the tied end of the string as Matt flicked it, jumping just as it was about to change course. Triumphant, clamping it in his mouth, he'd trot until the line couldn't stretch any farther, pulling him up short. Digging in his legs, he'd tug until the taut string flew out of his mouth, whipping back to hit the fence. Zero would sit back, waiting for just this moment. Rushing in, he'd bat the string that had escaped the grasp of his brother.

Oona came and went on her own schedule, disappearing impossibly until one evening when I was out front watering a plant I'd put by the front door. The sun was setting, and the light was reflecting off a flotilla of white clouds above New York. There was a breeze coming off the Hudson River, rustling through the leaves of the wall of trees across the street. The group of guys at the garage down the street, who had been fixing a pair of kids' bikes all day, had knocked off all pretense of work and were gossiping out in front of the battered metal door that was closed for the night.

Just as I turned to go back inside, I saw Oona emerge from the alleyway between Matt's house and Roberto's. She made a quick scan to ensure that no one was on the sidewalk and then scampered out, crouching under a car parked on the street. Walking by, you'd never notice her hiding behind the right back wheel. Her tail was pulled up around her body, her back low to the ground. In dusk, she looked like a bit of bunched-up paper or a discarded coffee cup.

She was preparing to cross the street. I glanced from her to the other side of the road. It seemed so close, but she was so small in comparison. She waited as cars streamed by in both directions, wheels rolling just a few feet from where she was hidden. She sat unmoving for five minutes. I became more and more apprehensive as the time stretched out, wanting her to turn back, wondering what she was waiting for. Cars swooshed up and down the block, though they weren't driving at their usual weekday breakneck speeds. Oona was patient, so focused on watching the automobiles that I worried that someone would come down the sidewalk and startle her. Would she run, despite the traffic? By now, I'd learned from the neighbors that cats were killed often on this road. Oona had survived this long because she was either lucky or smart. Watching her, I became convinced it had to be the second. Her ears flicked back and forth, taking in the sounds all around, and then with a leap, she sprinted forward, out in the open, paws skittering across the road. At just that moment, a car turned right at the far corner and started barreling down the street. I was about to yell, imagining the car hitting her, until, with three quick bounds, she dashed under the parked car on the other side of the street, safe for the time being.

How did she navigate this every day? I understood the lure of the wilderness in the Palisades, the steep basalt cliffs overgrown with trees, shrubs, and vines that separate Union City from the communities below that line the Hudson River. She didn't know how long she could count on us. She had to be careful to cultivate other food sources for herself and her kittens. One of the hardest things about helping the boys was realizing that Oona would be left outside alone after we trapped them. The best we could do was fix her and feed her. Forty-five minutes earlier, when Matt and I were watching the cats from the back door, that seemed like a lot, because the feline family appeared so happy. But as long as Oona lived outside, part of her life would include this road. I was terrified that one day, I'd find her dead in the middle of it.

As determined as I was to stay away from becoming loony tunes for cats, the bits and pieces I was learning from Joan and Matt's training fascinated me. When it comes to dealing with stray cats, three different groups of people emerge, each reflecting the personality of those taking on the tasks: trappers, fosterers, and feeders.

Trappers are your hotshots. They lug around big metal cages, are heartless about catching cats, and can handle the psychological experience of having three or four hulking feline shapes crouching in a state of constant anticipation in cages in their homes. Trappers catch the cats, haul them to the vet, and care for them for the two or three days after the operation. Being responsible for an animal in a trap, its mind whirring nonstop trying to figure out how to get free, is no mean feat. You get hissed at, swatted. Mistakes happen. Suffice to say that later in my rescuing career, when I became a trapper, not just one, but *two* ferals got out of the inescapable traps while on my watch in Matt's basement. Luckily, some tuna got them back in.

There are the fosterers. These are the folks who take in the kittens and friendly cats and find them homes. They seem cheery, happy to serve, like flight attendants on airplanes. Make no mistake: they're the enforcers. Their job is to pinpoint the humans who are good enough for their charges. The fosterers set up crates at local pet stores that they kit out with a small litter box, colorful toy, and hammock. Then, with an iron hand in a silk glove, they walk prospective adopters through the process, handing them forms to fill out, fixing adoption fees that keep the dilettantes at bay, arranging home visits, and setting traps to weed out the unworthy. "Under what circumstance would you declaw a cat?" they might ask. The unsuspecting respondent might say, "When my pet is in the process of destroying my three-thousand-dollar sofa." Wrong. *Never.* That's the answer. Because declawing comes down to amputating the end of the cat's toes at the last knuckle, chopping off bones and tendons. "Thanks for applying, but never is also when you'll get a cat from us."

Then, there is the last group, the one I learned the importance of while talking to Joan a couple of weeks after picking up the trap. We were in the final stages of preparing for our kitten-trapping D-day, and I had called Joan to get her advice about catching Oona once we had brought the boys in.

"Who's the feeder on your street?" Joan asked, after giving me the lowdown on what to expect after we took the kittens away. "You might want to make sure they don't also feed your mother when you decide to trap her. Just so that she's hungry enough to go into the trap."

"What feeder? Oona always shows up to eat like clockwork twice a day," I replied.

"Are there a lot of cats on your street?"

"Uh, yeah." That was like asking if there were a lot of muscle cars on Matt's block.

"You see the same group of cats around for the most part?" I could hear Joan's brain going into processing mode.

"Oh yes," I laughed. "We're in the land of black-and-white cats. I'm starting to recognize the familiar faces."

"Bets are there's a feeder somewhere nearby. If you notice the same ferals, there's usually someone putting out food for them. Cats are everywhere in our neighborhoods. Just part of where we live. But a group of regulars means someone is feeding them."

The notion of a feeder fascinated me. Feeders, on the front line, are the oddest piece of the cat-rescuing puzzle. These are the people who all too often creep out late at night or at the crack of dawn to put out plastic plates, tinfoil trays, and plastic carryout carriers filled with the weirdest assortment of what's on sale this week at Walmart. (Friskies at forty-nine cents a can is usually on the menu.) Invariably women, often emotional, feeders love their charges to distraction. Cats that would scratch your eyes out will inch up to rub against a feeder's legs before darting away. Too many make the grievous mistake of minding the cats without fixing them, because they can't bear to hurt the animals, only have enough money for food, or feel too isolated to reach out for help.

I hung up from my call with Joan, mystified. I was nearing obsession with wanting to catch one litter of kittens and put an end to their wandering life and my constant concern about them. What was it like to watch—and participate in—the whole thing continuing year after year? To feed cats every day and get to know their sweet faces the way I did Two Spot, Number Three, Zero, and Oona. Who could manage long term that feeling of responsibility and helplessness? I realized we had to find out who did in Matt's neighborhood, and soon, or we might not have a chance of catching Oona.

4

Our Fate Is Sealed

Everything was going as planned. Our assault was slated for the Fourth of July—just two weeks away. Matt had taken his class, we had the trap, the kittens were getting to know us. I should have known things were going too smoothly, that we were getting too comfortable with this cat-napping business.

Because that's exactly when Roberto appeared in the backyard with his machete, barbeque plans, and kiddie pool. In his attempt to salvage the situation and negotiate with Roberto to help him clean up, Matt managed to capture Number Three, but Two Spot and Zero were MIA. Now, I had to find a safe place to keep the kitten while Matt tried to locate the other two.

"I apologize for all of this, little guy. I promise you, we had something else in mind for this," I told Number Three, speaking through the pillowcase Matt had used to catch him in Roberto's backyard. I stepped into the kitchen, closed the sliding door, and went off in search of a dark closet.

You'd never think it, looking at the average domesticated cat stretched across a sofa, appropriating the entire piece of furniture, but when it comes down to it, a cat's favorite place in all the world is a small, dark, enclosed space. A feline disdains any outside attempts to control it. It whacks your hand when you try to scoot it off the couch, slumps immobile on your computer keyboard when you need it to move. Cats are domesticated, but only because about twelve thousand years ago they disdainfully (again) decided to tame themselves to get at the food those pesky humans were cooking around the fire and the mice it was attracting, certainly not to make any friends. Life runs on a cat's terms. It's what is so aggravatingly fascinating about them.

So it was surprising to me that everyone in the rescue world agreed that if you fling a sheet over a yowling cat ready to take your eye out for catching it in a trap, quiet and calm follows. Taking away their control, forcing them to just hunker down and focus on their breathing and their heartbeat like furry four-legged yogis seemed to slow them down like magic.

I climbed Matt's brick red lacquered stairs, a design element only an architect would think of, to the spare bedroom. I inched the closet door open. My feet disappeared under a monochrome puddle of brown, black, and gray T-shirts, a surefire sign that Matt, though he may live in New Jersey, still had the heart of a New Yorker. I kicked them aside and peeked in. Perfect.

I kneeled down, still holding on to the pillowcase with a

gentle grip. With my other hand, I took a few T-shirts that had fallen from the shelf and lined the hard floor, putting down just enough to make it more comfortable, but not enough to create a pile Number Three could hide under. I laid the pillowcase on the ground at the very back of the closet and moved the hole until it was right in front of Number Three so that he could wiggle out. With the pillowcase flattened on the floor and on top of him, I could see the outline of his little body.

I sat back on my heels and waited for him to come out.

He didn't move.

I waited five minutes, then ten.

He kept not moving.

Was he breathing? The problem with a dark closet was it was dark. I couldn't tell if his tiny lungs were working inside that minuscule chest. The rescue sites never mentioned this hitch. Of course, they also never mentioned any tips on how to rethink a planned rescue when faced with a machete-wielding neighbor.

Maybe Number Three had suffocated in the pillowcase?

Worried, I reached my hand over, picked up the end of the bag, and edged it back until it revealed two tiny paws, a pure white chest, and finally, Number Three's head.

He glared at me, doing his best to look terrifying. He didn't have a chance. Number Three, like his kitten brethren, was designed from the paws up to be adorable. His face was almost all white with just a splash of black on the top, as if he had been playing in paint and swiped his paw on his ear. His enormous round eyes, trying to stare me down, were a warm golden color. His ears were sweet triangles.

"We'll figure this out, don't you worry," I said to Number Three. He didn't move, his eyes glued to me as I closed the door.

Coming downstairs, I found Matt sitting in the kitchen.

"We're done. We didn't see the other kittens. I managed to guilt him into leaving them alone, talking about them as babies, telling him how crazy you were about them," he said. "We're going to have to wait until the barbeque is over and see if we can locate Two Spot and Zero."

This was a prime example of why I avoided doing things when I didn't know how they would end. I looked out the window, glanced at Matt, and sat next to him at the kitchen table. To wait. Why anyone opened themselves up to lack of control, this situation where anything could happen, was beyond me.

For the next half hour, we tracked every move that Roberto made, as if we were on a stakeout. Except, okay, Roberto wasn't doing anything illegal. We mouthed to each other what we figured the sounds going on out back were. *"He's setting up the grill."* *"He's brought out the radio."* *"He's blowing up the baby pool."* We eavesdropped as he called his brother and told him to come over for dinner around 5 P.M. Soon, the voices of his wife and child joined his, and we heard splashing, beers popping open, and chairs creaking as they settled in.

Matt turned to me. "This is going to be a long day," he said as he pulled me up by my shoulders and propelled me out of the kitchen.

We did what most people would do to distract themselves— we went shopping. Our choice? The pet store, to get some kitten food for Number Three. In the car, I pulled out my phone to call Yolanda at the vet just to see if, on an outside chance, we could keep Number Three.

"Wait till the mom comes back tonight and put him out," Yolanda said in a bright voice that brooked no discussion. "At six weeks, he's still too young. Eight weeks. That's what you're aiming for."

At PetSmart, we piled almost every type of kitten food there was into the cart. When we got home, we turned on a movie and waited.

I pretended to watch the screen, but I couldn't help thinking about Number Three upstairs, his little brothers outside. At least I hoped they were outside. What if they were hurt somewhere under all of that plywood and old furniture? Maybe that's why they hadn't come out. If it was fear that was making them hide, imagine how terrified they must be. Alone, scared to meow, not sure what had just hit them or what would happen next. That was just these kittens. What about all the other feral cats out there? What do they go through?

Fear was a big part of the rescue world, but the trick had to be to not let it overcome you. The only way I knew how to do that was to act. Maybe if I could find the feeder on our block, then I could see if I could handle taking care of some of the other cats so I wouldn't have to worry like this. Maybe if I found the feeder, sized up the situation, I could get a better understanding of just what doing something might mean. Whether I was the right one for the job. Perhaps the feeder would reveal all.

•   •   •

Right before sunset, we noticed something. Silence. Matt took a look out back. They were gone.

"Let's go on the roof," I suggested.

Matt and I ran upstairs and climbed up the ladder, throwing ourselves down on our stomachs on the black tar paper, searching down below.

Oona showed up right away on the wall above the yard. She must have been hiding anxiously nearby all day, waiting until she could come in and search for her babies. She jumped down, her normal caution forgotten, and paced around the shadows, checking out the foreign furniture, sniffing the cooler. She stood unmoving for a minute, a white wisp in the dusk, trying to gauge the safety of the area around her. Feral cats never stay out in the open in a strange situation. They skulk, they hide, they run away. She was acting out of desperation.

She mewled for the kittens. She repeated the low call, a plaintive sound. We watched, stretched out next to each other. Long minutes passed without any movement in the courtyard. This was what we had avoided talking about all day. As if not saying out loud what worried us—that the kittens might be hurt or might have escaped from Roberto's backyard and were wandering around, prey to the raccoons that came out at night—might keep it from happening. I reached over to take hold of Matt's hand.

Oona paced back and forth, her soft cry trailing behind her. She came to a halt, forlornly scanning the place she had chosen as a nursery for her children, a spot she had thought was safe but where, in the end, she'd been unable to protect them.

Then there was a sudden movement from behind the shed. Two kittens, a blur of black and white, dashed out to their mother. My eyes were wet, my hand clutched Matt's. How little I had believed this could work out, how much I thought the odds were stacked against them. I felt happier and luckier than I'd felt in a long time, grateful to the world and Matt for this unlikely outcome.

Matt climbed down the ladder and, ignoring Number Three's gruff hiss, stuffed him into a carrier he had found in the cellar. Out back, Matt placed the box, with its door ajar, at the entrance to Roberto's yard. Number Three waited a minute and then shot out of the carrier, jumping into the familiar mass of cat fur. As Oona nuzzled and licked the kittens, Zero collapsed happily on his back under her assault. They were just four wild cats, meaningless nothings to most people. But they were beautiful, reunited.

I turned out to be right about one bit of cat lore I'd been throwing around: mothers tend to act when their home is disturbed.

With the kittens reunited with Oona, it was a good time to have a beer, congratulate ourselves, and collapse into the chairs in the kitchen. Sitting there, I spied some movement out of the corner of my eye. White. Low to the ground. My newfound cat vision locked in. Oona was sauntering into Matt's yard like she belonged there. Crazier still, she was lugging a compliant Zero in her mouth.

"Oh boy, do you see that?" I whispered.

Matt stood up to get a look outside.

"No, no," I said, swatting my hand toward him while at the same time dropping down to my knees on the linoleum floor.

Matt's glance relayed just how crazy I looked at that moment, and he was right, because for some unknown reason I was suddenly convinced Oona would find me less threatening crouched on my knees rather than simply standing up the way she usually saw me. But at this point I was committed to the lower-to-the-ground notion.

Matt stooped into a reluctant half slouch. Then he caught sight of Oona, who was now marching toward the back flower bed, and his knees collapsed, mimicking my movement awkwardly like you do when you think the other person knows what they're up to even if your body doesn't recognize this new cat-hiding pose.

I later discovered that all the poses you end up in in cat rescue situations are weird because you are just creating them on the fly. Whether you're windmilling your arms to prevent a kitten that is bolting toward you from skedaddling out the bathroom door or splaying your limbs across the top of a drop trap to keep a gyroscoping feral cat you just caught from upending the cage, there's no dignity in cat rescuing. No matter what, the felines come out looking nimble and sleek and the humans like clumsy numskulls.

On our knees, we watched as Oona dropped Zero right on top of the hostas I had planted in the spring. She stared him down for a moment, and I could almost hear her telling him in a stern tone not to move or he would get a real tongue-lashing— as in a very forceful bath. She headed back across the concrete patio and disappeared through the hole in the fence to Roberto's now deserted mini-urban-beach-party. A few minutes later, she remerged with Two Spot's neck clamped between her teeth. Lanky Two Spot was a bit bigger than Zero, forcing Oona to drag his back legs along the ground as she walked back to the flower bed and Zero. Two Spot, ever obedient, didn't move an inch. He just let his legs dangle. At the edge of the bed, which was lined with bricks, she opened her mouth, and Two Spot landed in a pile next to Zero, crushing more hosta leaves. She turned around and headed back. At this rate, my hosta would be wiped out by the next kitten-sized delivery.

The wait dragged on. It shouldn't have surprised us. She was going after Number Three, and chances were, he was galloping around the yard in an impromptu game of catch the kitten. Finally, Oona reemerged, but this time, she was moving a lot more slowly. She had Number Three by the scruff of the neck—just barely. He was wriggling and squirming, trying to figure out where they were, where she was trying to take him, and how he could come out on top. He was so much bigger than the other two that she had to frog-march him toward his brothers, clamping onto his neck and dragging him forward. By the time they had reached the back of the yard, Oona had given up and released him. For a minute, I thought the hosta had a chance. Number

Three sprang up in the air like he was Tigger and crashed down on top of his brothers, rolling around for good measure.

Official Hosta Report: Dead on Number Three Arrival.

Then it hit me.

I turned to Matt. He swung toward me.

"We have kittens," we whispered to each other.

Those next few hours marked the moment we toppled down the rabbit hole, when our fate was sealed. Attending a cat rescue workshop was sort of like a shot over the bow, but you could also argue that it was just good old-fashioned curiosity. What New Yorker didn't want to know more about the odd subcultures that make their city idiosyncratic? And, okay, today had been pretty intense, what with the machete, the kitten in the pillowcase, lying in wait for Oona on the roof. But again, we were just reacting to the situation at hand as best we could.

What happened next confirmed that we, or at least I, for the moment, had the inner makings of a real crazy cat person. Because after this point, everything was voluntary, deliberate, and done out of that final loony step—trying to read the feline mind. Many have attempted and failed, but that never stopped the next cat-hair-covered person from looking deeply into their pet's elliptical eyes for a sign, any sign, of what the critter wanted.

"This is great," said Matt, rising on one knee to get up and reaching over to grab his beer off the counter. "Now we don't have to worry about them for the next couple of weeks."

I clutched his arm and pulled him back down.

"What are you doing?" I whispered in a harsh tone, pulling Matt along with me in an awkward, low shuffle to the right. When we were out of sight of his big glass back door, I collapsed next to the table.

"What . . ." Matt began.

I interrupted him. He didn't get it yet. "We won't have to worry about them if we can make them stay."

"I'm sure they'll stay. Anyway, they're cats. Wild cats, last time I checked. You can't make them do anything."

"Of course you can't make them. But we can make it so that they want to stay."

"Relaxing music?"

"Matt."

"Okay, what?"

What indeed. What would a cat like? I tried to think. Well, after the day they just had, a good place to start was peace and quiet. I looked around, and then it dawned on me.

"The sliding door," I said.

"What about the sliding door?" Matt asked, examining it for potential cat appeal.

"We need to cover it up."

"Cover up a sliding door? Why?"

"Because of that," I said, pointing up at the ceiling.

"It's a light."

"Exactly."

He waited a minute, looking at me with a questioning gaze. "And?"

I couldn't believe it wasn't obvious to him.

"It's getting dark, and the light will shine right on them all night. What cat wants that? If I were Oona, lying there all night with a light in my eyes, I'd find something better."

"Heather, they live in backyards . . . in the city." He said the last part in a slow, deliberate way. "Their life is drowning in lights."

"If you want to risk driving them away with all this light after the day we just had, that's your choice. But I'm not going along." I went off in search of some type of covering.

Matt may have been perplexed, but he wasn't dumb. He knew his best bet was to just ride this out. When I reemerged with a black sheet from upstairs, he was ready with duct tape and a hammer. As he watched me unfold the fabric, he chose the duct tape as his tool of choice.

I'm still not sure how we got the cloth up, since I insisted on turning out the lights, not just in the kitchen, but across the whole downstairs, which meant we had to work in total darkness. I also decreed that we couldn't just walk in front of the door. Somehow, I crawled across the floor, holding a corner of the cloth and a stepladder. On the other end of the sliding door, Matt crouched until I gave the signal, and then we both stood, the sheet stretched between us. At one point, I had the fabric between my teeth as Matt leaned over to hand me some duct tape. Eventually, the covering was up. A little crooked, but we had achieved blackout mode.

"Okay, so that's done," Matt said, his voice disembodied in the now pitch-dark kitchen. "I'm starved."

I thought for a moment.

"Let's go out. You shouldn't use this room for the next couple of weeks, okay? Because of the noise."

Matt was silent in the dark, but I heard his brain working. Hanging sheets, crouching around in the shadows. There was a balance we were working on here, but neither of us had any experience with what might end up tipping us over.

Matt got me. Where other people noticed how I hung my pictures at home on the wall with such precision and saw someone who liked symmetry, Matt recognized it for the orderly looniness that it was. I felt things deeply, and sometimes that paralyzed me, but it also made me make sudden huge commitments, and attempts to arrange everything in the ways I thought were right. He didn't enable me. He was quick to tell me that ranting about the stupidity of the city planting trees along the street that weren't native to the area and that didn't help the birds or the insects was not the best use of my energy. But he recognized that my desire to do the right thing—and sometimes force other people to do it, too—was part of what made me the person he loved.

It was nice to be outed. A relief to be known and understood, in all your craziness and glory.

With the cat project, I found myself relying more and more on this thing Matt and I were constructing between us, this relationship that neither of us had fully committed to. I was relying on his logical, measured counterweight to balance out my innate need to exert control over this entire situation. You can't have authority over cats, especially feral ones.

This could all blow up in our faces. I could start trying to exert control over this cat situation to the point that I ended up taking out my inevitable frustrations on my relationship with Matt. I knew that part of myself, the damage I was capable of. Too often in the past, the flip side of my need to control has been disappointment and recriminations. There's a balance you need when you decide to exert your will, one I hadn't mastered. When things didn't turn out as planned, I was too quick sometimes, because I was so disappointed, to blame myself and others. In my need to do right, I could end up shutting Matt out. What, after all, was the line between quarantining your kitchen and looking after some cats?

Tricky indeed.

For the moment, Matt was done arguing. Even though he knew it meant a twenty-minute walk down the hill to Hoboken for dinner.

5

Standard Operating Procedure

Having cats over as our permanent backyard residents changed everything. When they lived next door, I couldn't track their every move. A plate of food every morning and afternoon, a little spying from the roof, but no tugs at my heartstrings every time Number Three tried to climb the trellis in the backyard only to slide into a puddle on top of Zero. No scolding huffs each time Two Spot destroyed yet another of my hosta leaves with a swat of his mischievous paw.

Now, I felt responsible for their every comfort. It was as if we had become a B and B that pampers its guests—right before kidnapping them for their own good. As an added bonus, all our services were discreetly hidden behind a lopsided curtain stuck to the wall over the sliding glass doors with silver duct tape. Still, what was surprising was how dramatic the life of an outdoor kitten could be. It seemed like it should just be lazing about, drinking milk, playing with your brothers. Yet, it could be hard.

It started to rain. Not the light, misty kiss-your-cheek rain they get in Seattle. We had downpours that just wouldn't stop. It was like the metropolitan area was going through its own monsoon season. Normally, I love the rain. I made the decision when I was around ten or so that I adored it, and I never wavered, even when I lived in Paris, where it continuously rains after the cold weather sets in and you're perpetually in danger of losing your eye to the packs of tiny, elderly French ladies with umbrellas who will run you down if you don't jump out of their path.

Three days of unrelenting storms, pelting day and night, might not have gotten to me before, as I skipped across the puddles in New York between work and home, feeling cool in my new pair of blue Hunter boots. But all thoughts of competitive dressing seemed silly when I started to worry, wondering how the cats were holding up.

Arriving at Matt's house that Friday night, the answer was, they were wet. Oona had them tucked under the wooden stairs leading down from Matt's concrete deck to the little patio below. That provided some protection. But when Matt opened the sliding glass door to slip a heaping plate of food under the sheet to them and they scampered up to eat, they got soaked in less than half a minute.

I looked down at them in the fading evening light. Their white coats were plastered to their little baby bodies. They were cuter than ever. With their downy fur slicked close, you could see just how round their little tummies were. They looked like white seals, with tubby middles and stubby, flipper-like legs. But then Zero opened his mouth wide and sneezed, almost collapsing back on his hind legs, a surprised look on his face. When he was stable once more, he shook his head and started eating again.

"He keeps doing that," Matt said, shaking his own head in sympathy.

Did he seem a little slower? Was his head nodding a bit? This was the problem. I could worry nonstop now that Zero was living behind Matt's house. Zero was the kind of kitten you would baby, even when he wasn't sick. He was smaller than his brothers, a round ball of fluff that always stuck a bit closer to Oona. He played hard but wound up at the bottom of the kitten pile or loping behind the other two.

"Yolanda won't let us catch them," I said, frustrated by, but also admiring of, one receptionist's sway over us. "What can we do?"

It's worth mentioning that at this point, we were on our knees, whispering to each other, peeping around the edges of the sheet as the kitchen got darker because we didn't turn the lights on in the kitchen anymore after sunset. Just your regular hotel-visitor consideration.

"I have an idea," Matt whispered.

And that was how we ended up building a cat house.

Constructing a home for a stray may seem the definition of cat obsession. But it's standard operating procedure in the rescue community. Maybe we all just feel bad for putting them through the ovary-removal and testicle-snipping business. In exchange for that little inconvenience, we give them a home.

I am not talking ordinary wooden boxes. Nothing seems to stir the creativity of feline fanatics like coming up with a home for their creatures—even if those animals would as soon swipe you in the eye as come near you.

Kitty habitat options run the gamut from single dwellings to cabins to, this being the city, catominiums. Shelters are often insulated, heated, and painted. They're made out of disposable coolers, the plastic storage tubs you buy at Home Depot, those faux rocks used in parks to cover up pool equipment, wood shipping pallets, camper toppers, even foam planters turned upside down. They sport heating pads, low-watt lightbulbs, breezeways, slanted roofs, overhanging porches, heated water bowls, Plexiglas windows so the cats can scope out the landscape, and sometimes even curtains. Since rescuing is becoming trendy, architects are getting into the mix, running contests with local rescue groups to build evocative, minimalist concept shelters, complete with shag covering and radio transmitters to track how long a cat uses the house and how much it weighs.

It's as if when it comes to the houses, people just let loose. These creatures inspire such compassion and guilt. You can't give them that much or bridge the gap between the wild lives that they live and the pampered ones that indoor cats have—except with a shelter.

That was exactly the way that Matt approached our cat house. For him, creating a structure, even a cat-sized one, wasn't a project to be undertaken lightly. Matt was an architect—designing buildings was what he did. What it came down to, really, was that he was part of this shifting world of contradictions that we non-architects can never understand.

In my experience, an architect is someone who writes lists in impressively concise, careful handwriting—and then loses the list. Always. Never buy kitchen utensils for architects. As a breed, they obsess over culinary items, so there is no possible way you can buy the *right* Japanese sushi knife. Not to mention that it's also a waste of money to splurge on that modern white porcelain bird-shaped soy sauce container you are thinking of buying because your architect friend said she liked it. Architects are too busy spending time at the office to ever use anything at home. Their house is just a notion to them.

To me, Matt and his ilk were this confusing mix of right brain and left brain. One minute, I'd think he was a rational geek, as I watched him trying to figure out the most efficient way to cut up his Christmas tree after the holidays so he could compost it. Next thing I knew, he was leaning it up in the back corner of his yard just so, having decided that it would be a good tree for the birds to hide in during the winter. There the spruce stood until April, changing from green to a burnt orange yellow.

A building project is never something to be taken lightly. Each one defines the architect. Which is why some are notorious for taking forever to remodel or build their own homes. They stall out trying to find exactly the right half-inch pentagon-shaped tiles for the bathroom or someone to hand mill their front door.

I, on the other hand, was more the identify-the-task-and-then-get-it-done kind of person. I didn't let projects drag on. To me, an unfinished project was an admission of failure. The essential difference in approach between Matt and me bewildered and frustrated me, causing me to wonder when we were in the middle of a fight why we were together.

That's why I was relieved about the cat house project. Because (1) it was small and (2) we needed it right away. That last point was made clear the next Saturday morning when we woke up, looked out the window of Matt's bedroom, and saw what appeared to be buckets of water being tossed off the roof.

"Let's go," I said, swinging out of bed intent on finding a hammer and some wood.

"Okay," responded Matt, sitting up and pulling open the drawer of the table next to him to get out a notebook and a Sharpie.

Here we go.

After breakfast, Matt spent a good half hour drawing. Finally, I couldn't help it anymore.

"We are just talking about a box, right?" I joked.

He looked up, perplexed by what I meant.

"I'm trying out a few ideas," he said, turning the paper in my direction. "We need to make sure there is ventilation," he explained, pointing at some holes in one drawing. "Good runoff for the rain," he added, hovering the pen over what looked like a cantilevered roof.

Ventilation? Puzzled, I gazed down. I looked back up, understanding once again why he was deliberate. Where I imagined a box for staying out of the rain, he saw a place where the cats could be comfortable, not just shut in. Also, I noticed he had included a floor, which hadn't been part of my mental design. Floors, when it was wet, I realized, was an insightful strategic move.

"It's good. I like it," I said.

"Which one?" he asked.

"Err, can't you just smash them together? Do all of your best ideas at once?"

He gave me that perplexed look again, like he couldn't tell if I was serious or not.

Matt kept drawing. And he kept drawing. Finally, he decided on his plan and showed it to me. Fairly simple, after all that, with a raised floor, a flat roof, ventilation slots on the sides, and a wide-open front, but thoughtful, thorough. He headed down to the basement to find some wood and start sawing.

I was still in my admiring mode, though my impatience was growing. Didn't he understand how urgent it was to get a roof over their heads? It was pouring outside. If Zero got any sicker, it would be our fault because we had had the chance to help him. I tried to settle down with the Saturday *New York Times* and just let Matt be in charge here. After much foraging, I had discovered that the corner store five blocks away (in New York you would call it a bodega because these shops are typically run by Hispanics, but in Union City where pretty much everyone was Hispanic, a distinction like that made no sense) had exactly five copies for sale on weekend mornings. Never an early riser, I made sure to get up around eight on the weekends I was at Matt's.

Still, I couldn't help myself from heading down to the basement every so often. Each time, he was sawing or standing back and considering the wood with an intense look on his face, which

I tried to find reassuring. But how long does cutting take? I would have had the thing done and outside by now, and the cats wouldn't still be wet.

Around three o'clock, Matt emerged from the basement.

"Done?" I asked, excited about the idea of seeing little bodies running into and out of, but mostly into, the house.

"I need to go buy some more wood," he responded. "I don't think it's big enough, now that I cut the pieces and laid them out."

My frustration with him, which had been on a slow simmer, boiled up fast. We were talking about a cat house. Not the Empire State Building or Fallingwater.

"All they need is someplace to get out of the rain. Look at it outside, it's awful."

"It's not right," he said calmly.

"Why don't you just put it together and put it out there now and see if works?"

"You can't put it out and then move it again. These are outdoor cats. It will take them a while to get used to one new home without switching it on them."

I stood there staring at him, amazed we were arguing about a mini house. Though it was a lot more than that. The random stuff he collected drove me batty, but he couldn't imagine living without it. Then there were the looming questions about Union City: Why would he choose to live here? Would I ever make that choice to live here with him? To me, it was isolated, a deliberate move he had made to be away from people. How were two people who had such different approaches to doing things and to where they felt they belonged supposed to work together?

Matt's affection for piling up stuff all over the place, whether it was mail or unused nails, and his ability to get lost in arcane activities, like this house, was foreign to me. It made me wonder how he ever got anything done, whether he was ambitious enough to be a good partner.

For me, order and action driven by worry: those were the ways to get ahead, to get things done. But Matt didn't seem to fret over anything. Even now, he looked unperturbed, although he was talking about starting from scratch while the cats shivered in the backyard.

"It's important for it to be the right place for them," Matt said, smiling to me as he grabbed the keys and headed out.

He hadn't given me the time to switch from frustration to anger, and now I was standing there staring at the door.

I looked back down at the paper, full of news about New York and all the important, driven people right across the river. Matt had headed out into the rain (having forgotten his raincoat, of course, so he would come home soaked) to Home Depot (where he would get lost because he hated asking where things were) to get wood for a shelter for cats that I wanted to save.

How much was he interested in the whole rescue effort personally? I wasn't sure. The community trapping program he'd learned about at Neighborhood Cats had intrigued him, but he was still torn, wondering how much better off the kittens would be in our clumsy care. Based on all of this, I could only conclude he was doing all of this work for me, not the cats.

It was his go-with-the-flow attitude that made that possible. If I wasn't completely committed to a project as time-consuming and nerve-racking as rescuing kittens, I definitely wouldn't be as supportive. Each to his own, that had been my motto for many years, because for many years that was how I had always thought of myself. On my own. But Matt, without hesitating, had jumped in to support me, regardless of what I had asked of him. It was important to me, the person he loved, so he made it important to him, too.

When I first started seeing my therapist, Susan, she pushed me to put together a mental list of what I felt I was missing in life. She called it a bag of goodies. I let that phrase put me off of trying to come up with this list for a while. Susan liked to use clichés, and I liked to think that meant she wasn't clever enough to get me. Isn't a therapist supposed to utter more profound things than "the grass is always greener on the other side," and "a bird in the hand is worth two in the bush"? Once I even counted up how many clichés she used during our forty-five-minute session (eight) as retaliation for her obsession with me coming up with my "bag of goodies." But then Susan began to get me to understand that my dependency on work grew from my tendency to let the world around me define what I expected out of myself. That my fear of commitment came from the fact that I'd never experimented with intimacy, never allowed myself to be dependent. That failure was part of the learning process. I discovered (*surprise!*) that I was wrong. Susan was one of the most insightful people I knew. Don't judge a book by its cover, indeed.

After that, I finally came up with that list for Susan. Matt, well, maybe not by name, but the vague idea of a boyfriend, had been at the top. It wasn't that I wanted someone to have children with.

Frankly, I couldn't imagine ever being able to handle being responsible for creating a life so totally dependent on me. I had plenty of friends who sought out love so they could start a family, but that was the furthest idea from my mind. No, it's more that I was willing to admit that I finally wanted to see what it was like to be in love and be vulnerable, to find someone who I could be happy and sad with. I wanted to figure out what made a man I was crazy about tick, what made him the person he was. I wanted to care for someone who cared for the person I was becoming. After I met Matt, I worked with Susan, step-by-step, to push through my insecurities about failure, to resist my urge to punt at the first signs (real or imagined, it hadn't mattered) of doubt. I stuck to him, in love, but we were so different that I was also often confused.

And now, here we were. One of the things I appreciated, even as it puzzled me, was how accepting and patient Matt was. Part of loving someone, I was learning, wasn't just understanding and caring about what made that person who he or she was. It was sharing those cares. When I was up or down, irrational or not, he cut me slack. He gave me room to make decisions and move at my own pace. He was willing to go along to see how things went. He had faith. After all these years alone, did I have it in me to learn to give him that same consideration?

When Matt returned, he was wet (as predicted) and loaded down with enough boards to make ten cat-family houses. "Remember I was talking about wanting to expand the roof garden, so I could have more tomato plants and you could put in some flowers?" he exclaimed, lugging the wood into the house.

Matt goes out for a few boards and comes back with makings for a rooftop extravaganza. Classic.

"I also got burritos, so we can eat and then I'll tackle the cat house," he added, as he set the boards down in the middle of the living room.

Again, classic. Matt is incapable of passing up any opportunity to eat Mexican food, the spicier the better. There's a good Mexican joint on the route back from Home Depot. Was that why he had gone out in the first place? Not for the first time, I wondered if proximity to authentic Latin American cuisine was a strong reason why he chose Union City, which is 80 percent Latino.

After the hour I had spent waiting for Matt, I was determined to try to still my instinct to organize. That wasn't easy with that pile of wood just sitting there, begging to be put down in the basement. But, I had to start somewhere, and an inanimate stack of planks was as good a place as any. We had dinner. It was delicious. I focused on that. The cats had dinner. I decided to be happy for that. They didn't get wet for the first time in a week because there was a bit of a break in the weather and it stopped raining, though the clouds didn't seem to be in any hurry to move along.

After eating, Matt went to the basement to cut the boards. I wandered down the steps an hour later, only to find that he had cut all the wood with a handsaw. His jigsaw blade had become too dull. Apart from some blisters and an apology to me for taking so long, he didn't seem bothered. I'd never fully under-stand this aspect of his personality. I didn't have to. I just had to accept it.

With the cutting over, Matt was ready to start nailing. *Wham, wham.* The hammer blows echoed throughout the little base-ment. Enough to maybe make a mother cat, already a little gun-shy, think about moving house.

He looked up at me.

"Too loud, right?" he said, as if reading my mind. There was a little window on the west side of the basement right next to the patio steps out back. Oona and the kittens had to hear every single hammer blow.

Wham. Matt tried it again just to be sure.

"That won't work," I agreed.

We trudged upstairs, lugging the pieces of wood with us. The first floor, a big space open from the front hallway to the kitch-en's sliding back door, wasn't right, either.

Matt opened the front door. It had started raining again. But there was a little metal overhang over the front porch. He beck-oned to me. I brought the pieces I was carrying outside.

It was soaked and dark. The only movement was the traffic on the street.

Saturday night. Nine o'clock. Pouring rain. On the street. Matt was hammering.

I looked around. Nobody was out, but the thuds were deafen-ing, and the buildings on his block were stuck side by side. I may have been becoming more accepting, but I was still going to try to arrange things.

85

"Do you think you can do that less loudly?" I asked after he finished hammering another nail.

Matt looked up.

"You want me to hammer quietly?"

I gazed back and waved my hand at Juan and Lydia's door. "Yeah," I said. "You know, the neighbors."

Matt just sighed and started hammering again.

The house? It was perfect, of course. We put it out the next morning, using the food plate as bait. It didn't take long. Oona never missed a detail. She saw the plate and trotted up the steps. Though it was pouring, she moved cautiously, sniffing the front corners of the house, just poking her nose inside. She drew her head back and looked around the entire yard. Now pretty damp, she inched one paw at a time into the box. I peeked over at Matt to see if he looked as worried as I felt. I held my breath until she stopped and poked her head back out, checking out the patio again. Just like that, perimeter search over, she stepped inside, dipped her head down, and started eating.

Several long moments passed. Oona lifted her head and meowed for the kittens. Within a couple of minutes, the house was full of cats out of the rain. All we heard was the crunching of dry food on the other side of the sliding glass door followed after a while by silence. Peeking around the edge of the curtain, we could see that instead of shooing them outside the box and down the steps, Oona turned toward the kittens. She started licking Two Spot's right ear, pushing so hard that the left ear went flat against his head.

We watched as she washed each kitten in turn, drying Zero off with a long bath and giving a wriggling Number Three a quick once-over. I giggled when she lay down and the kittens moved in next to her to sleep, bumping against one another as they settled in. Matt and I had an official cat house, complete with cats.

6

So *This* Is Union City

Communities are like families. A single dinner or movie outing isn't going to tell you much about them. You need an all-day holiday affair—like Thanksgiving, with lots of awkward bumping into one another in the kitchen, small talk that, without any warning, veers into a knock-down-drag-out over who snubbed whom in the past, and a little too much wine over turkey—for all of the weird ticks, anxieties, and unexpected kindnesses of family, friends, and neighbors to really come out. You don't build the kind of trust in people that guarantees you will be able to bounce back from misunderstandings or accept one another's faults until you have spent time simply watching one another's rhythms.

I was in Union City every weekend and, as a result, was starting to understand the place—at least a little bit. Not that it was suddenly this Broadway show with a big reveal where the citizens emerged dancing in the street. It was just that I was getting keyed into the pace of the place. Then, as if a signal that I didn't understand had sounded, or I had passed some enigmatic test, the neighbors started to pay attention to me. Having scoped me out, seen me sweeping the front stoop or heading to the bus stop in the morning, they started to greet me with a sort of half nod. The next step was a strong hello and maybe a comment or two about the weather. (If you were Latino, you'd get an *"Hola"* or *"Buenas."* But we were so obviously of the Waspy white extraction that no one ever tried that out on us.) That was Union City. The people who live here, stay here. They make it their business to know one another's lives. It's very much a live and let live neighborhood. But it's a small-town attitude, where you believe you have the right to know and talk about everyone's business. And, evidently, I had been judged worth knowing.

Sure enough, a week after we brought home Joan's trap, such a moment came when I was out front, dumping the trash into the cans there. Matt's neighbor Marjie was on her stoop two doors down, using a gray watering can to splash some petunias that she had planted in her beige plastic flower boxes. Marjie is diminutive, curvy, and bubbly, with the long swing of dark hair that seems to be a prerequisite for living in New Jersey. I could easily imagine her out dancing every night. Except that, married straight out of Union City High School, she was a homebody with three teenage boys to feed and keep in line. When you looked through their front windows in the early evening, you could see the whole family sitting in the front room on a black leather couch and in big blue chairs, framed on one side by a big-screen TV and on the other by a thirty-inch-by-forty-inch photo of Marjie in a white strapless satin dress standing next to her husband, Will, massive in a black suit, on their wedding day.

"Hi," Marjie said, waving a free hand. She had a rich way of talking that sounded like she was always on the verge of laughter.

"Hi," I replied, taking a few steps down the sidewalk to her, uncertain whether this was a come-on-over or a good-to-see-you, stay-where-you-are wave.

Gesturing to the red, blue, and yellow striped espadrilles I was wearing, she said, "Those look just like shoes from my country."

I'd only spoken to Marjie a few times, but I knew she was talking about Ecuador, even though she was born and raised in Union City. What she was referring to was the country her mother was from. It was what people said. Juan, who emigrated from the Dominican Republic but was an American citizen and had been here for over half of his life, talked about the DR as his country. It's not as if they didn't consider themselves Americans or a part of Union City, they just had a broader sense of their communal network.

This was an odd concept to me, as a person who had moved so often and cut so many ties, a person who believed that the best way to be accepted in a new place was to jettison my old self and adapt. My experience was that keeping up with the past too much only ended up making a muddle of the person I was trying to become to fit in. It was a habit to let the tethers slip because I believed I could always replace a friend I missed or a group I felt a part of, though often imperfectly.

"I saw that cage you had the other day," Marjie said without warning, putting her watering can down on the concrete steps of her brick stoop. "What's it for?"

I looked at her for a moment, trying to smile while in fact I was panicking. Are we in trouble? Is she going to complain? I hadn't seen her on the street when we had come home with the trap last weekend after picking it up at Joan's house. My mind skittered about, trying to pick among a few different responses: Home decorating? New kind of planter? I knew what we planned to do was foreign around here. The cat books talk about the fine line between getting people on your side and not drawing too much attention to your activities. After the fiasco with Roberto, we did need to catch up on our community relations so none of the neighbors would call animal control by mistake. If ever there was a time to be honest, it was now that we'd been spied bringing a giant metal cage into the house.

Marjie looked at me expectantly, not talking for the moment, which wasn't like her. Marjie usually kept up a nonstop flow of conversation. I would later learn that her modus operandi was to ask you a question and then launch into a whole other train of thought, as though the most efficient thing was to get two conversations taken care of at once. This silence, paired with that searching look on her face, was unnerving. Until I realized that that look on her face was just curiosity.

"We're going to catch some kittens," I said slowly.

"Kittens!" she exclaimed. Her face lit up with exactly the same expression people have when they talk about newborn babies. Very good sign. "You mean the kittens in your backyard?"

I stared at her.

"Roberto told me about them, how they've moved into your backyard. He can see them from his back window."

Of course he could, I realized, and of course she knew.

"There are three, right?"

I bet she even knew what colors they were and their names.

"Uh, right," I managed to stutter. "We've been watching them for a few weeks in Roberto's backyard. I mean, before they moved to ours. We borrowed that trap so we can catch them next week."

"That's great!" Marjie enthused.

I was shocked.

"We have cats wandering through our backyard all the time. I never thought of catching them. Is it hard?"

I gave her a quick rundown about how you trapped and tamed kittens.

"At least in theory, that's how it works," I added. "We haven't done it yet."

"Let me know how it goes," she encouraged, picking up her watering can and turning to go into the house. That was that. Union City. Know what people are up to, but live and let live.

We also told Juan and Lydia, Matt's other next-door neighbors, just in case they saw us feeding the kittens. They had lived in the neighborhood forever, buying their house by saving money over the years from his job on a loading dock and hers as a community college secretary. Juan, a round man, smelling sweetly of cologne, loved to sit out front in the evening, the blue mosquito zapper hanging on his gate going about its business as he chatted with neighbors, who all confided their problems to his open, accepting gaze. Lydia, who was even stouter than Juan and wore a parade of below-the-knee matronly skirts, seemed more restrained at first. But get her started and you were in for a good half-hour gossip session about the neighbors, although her view always seemed spiked with more shrewdness than her husband's.

It was from Lydia, for instance, that I got the lowdown about the woman who had lived across the street in the now-abandoned redbrick house that sat behind a tall wooden fence with the word *PEACE* painted across it in fading purple and green letters. No surprise, the woman, Mary, had been a hippie who would stand in her bathrobe on her front step when she went out to get the paper, smiling and waving when Lydia was on her way to work. "Very kind lady," Lydia explained. "Smart," she added, in the next breath. She was smart because that old hippie had sold her place near the top of the real estate bubble to a group of big-time developers eager to exploit her tract of land on the cliffs overlooking the New York skyline.

Lydia also confided in me her suspicion that Marco, our neighbor three doors down with the brilliant blue green eyes and slight slouch, was a major drug dealer. She let the speculation slip one hot evening, as the traffic lined up down the block the way it does on some weekend nights, an impatient pileup of headlights and the occasional shock of a horn ten feet away. I just stared at her, surprised that she was talking about something more urgent than the mosquitoes, the traffic, and Juan's shoulder problems, which usually dominated our conversations. She nodded as if my inability to respond summed up the severity of the situation.

"There are always cars waiting outside his house. We need to keep an eye on him," she told me.

We had moved to the higher ground of neighborhood security. I was being drawn into the circle. I dutifully reported this tidbit to Matt.

"If Marco is such a big-time drug lord, why's he living in a run-down railroad rental apartment with his wife and three daughters?" Matt replied with a big dose of skepticism.

Which, you had to admit, was a good point, but one I knew Lydia would ignore. Good gossip is too hard to give up.

When I told Lydia about the kittens one evening as I stood chatting with them outside their front gate, beyond a quiet, "Oh really?" her reaction was polite acceptance without any further comment. If I'd explained Matt was planning to redo his house with pink plastic siding, she'd think it wasn't her place to say anything beyond a "That's nice, dear."

Juan looked on quizzically, knowing full well from my face that though Lydia wasn't saying much, I'd just imparted some key bit of information. Lydia translated our intentions to him in Spanish. After she finished, he nodded and then said something back.

"He says we'll let you know if we see any other kittens. They're usually some in the lot across the street this time of year."

I smiled, stoic. Wonderful. Now they think we're the official cat people. Still, I was grateful that they were okay with the notion, though I didn't want to tell Juan and Lydia how wrong they were. We hadn't elected ourselves to cat office.

Then there was Tony. Now that I had started telling people, I couldn't seem to stop confessing left and right. Matt's neighborhood was intimate, but the divisions were clear. On the east side, overlooking the Palisades and the million-dollar view of New York City, were the big homes where the older Italians or Germans who had moved here in the 1950s lived. On the west side of the street, Matt's side, were the beat-up row houses and the Hispanic families. Tony and his wife, Pat, had lived in a house on the nicer side of the street for fifty years. They were a classic New Jersey German-Italian pairing of the Catholic kind. They knew the block better than anyone and spent a lot of time outside their front gate, taking out the trash, walking up and down the block, making sure they kept up with what was what.

Tony and Pat liked gossiping and doling out advice. Pat greeted each new holiday with an array of decorations outside her front door—a foam ghost and plastic jack-o'-lantern at Halloween, pale eggs hung with ribbons on the bush out front at Easter. Tony spent most of his time lugging home a collection of junk that included everything from faded yellow plastic milk crates to concrete statues of saints.

I didn't need to tell them about our plans; Tony and Pat lived down the block on the other side of the street. But when Matt and I walked down the hill to Hoboken sometimes, to take the ferry to work on Monday mornings, we'd run into Tony, and he was always chatty, giving us pointers we never asked for. So one weekend, when I was out for a walk, he and I started talking. I brought up how we'd found some kittens in our backyard and how we planned to trap them. I joked about the workshop Matt had gone to and how he'd been told that there were likely a lot of cats around here that should probably be trapped and fixed.

Tony's reaction was instant and negative.

"Why would anyone want to do a silly thing like that?"

"Well," I paused. After how easy it had been to talk to Juan, Lydia, and Marjie about the kittens and trapping, I wasn't pre-pared for pushback. Especially from Tony, who I had pegged as bossy rather than critical. "I-I think people think it's the humane thing to do, so that the cats don't have any more kittens."

"We like the cats," Tony replied.

I see. I must not have done a good job at explaining.

"These people don't hurt the cats, Tony," I said.

"They won't have any more kittens, so there will be fewer of them after a while."

"Yeah," I nodded. "That's kind of the point."

We stood for a minute, not looking at each other. He was silent, but I could hear him in my head clucking his tongue at me, which corresponded well, since Tony, short, compact, and inquisitive, looked like a barnyard rooster.

"That's nonsense. Cats having kittens, being outside, it's the law of nature," Tony said, staring straight at me as if he could berate me into agreeing with him. His back was stiff with disap-proval, making his chest stick out more than usual. He was conflicted. He wanted to give me kind advice and yet because I wasn't agreeing with him, he wanted to bend me to his will. "What would we do about the mice if someone took them and did this to them?"

Now I get it. Most people don't like trapping because they think it encourages the cats to hang around, eat, and pee. Most people just want the cats gone. Tony wasn't most folks. He wanted them around to chase away the mice. He believed they were and should stay wild. He didn't like that fixing them meant there would be fewer of them. Tony understood trapping better than most people. Maybe there was more to this than that he just wanted the cats on the Palisades to stick around. Perhaps he and Pat were the feeders? He'd gotten upset fast enough for me to think that had to be the case.

"You're not planning on doing this yourselves, are you?" he said.

I looked up, realizing we'd both been silent for a moment. What was behind those words was the look he was giving me. Tony didn't say it, but I bet he suspected that people who trapped cats must take them away and dump them somewhere. That was what he did with the raccoons and groundhogs that wandered across his property. He'd already boasted to me that one year alone, scores of unsuspecting critters found themselves moving unexpectedly to the Meadowlands. It was better for them, he had assured me, to be away from the cars and out in a bigger space. I think it just gave him something to do.

"No, Tony. We just want to catch the kittens in our backyard to help them. To find them homes."

"Well, then, it's not worth talking about," he said, relaxing his stance. "You should help those kittens. It's a good thing to do." With that, he moved on to complaining about how hard it was some nights to get a parking space on the street and giving me inside information about where to find a place up the road.

Tony and I never talked about cats again after that.

I started asking around whether people knew if there was someone on the block who fed cats. I didn't ask if it was Tony. But I had to know. Knowing this would help me decide what to do. If the feeders turned out to be Tony and Pat, we would have reached a dead end. Because any trapping we would to do of adult cats, if we opted for that, could only happen with their involvement. It wouldn't happen if Tony had any say in the matter. If it were someone else, someone we could sway to our cause, maybe understanding their motivations and their goals would help me understand what I wanted to make not just of the strays, but of Matt, of this place, and of myself.

It was at this point that our kitten-trapping plan took another wild turn. We had the cats right where we wanted them. Then, like the wily felines they were, they took matters into their own paws. During the day, like any other parent with a steady job, Oona would have breakfast with the kids. In her case, it was a few healthy mouthfuls of wet food on top of piles of dry kibble all swimming in a pool of KMR. KMR, a white, syrupy fake kitten milk, is irresistible to cats of all ages. It comes in a blue and white pop-open can with an adorable pug-nosed Siamese kitten on the front. It's made for orphan kittens, one- to four-week-old little bits that can't eat solid foods yet. You feed abandoned kittens using an eyedropper or a miniature bottle and nipple. Which was just too cute until I realized, after doing further reading online, that taking care of a palm-sized one- or two-week-old kitten means feeding it every two hours—around the clock. It's like going through the exhaustion of early child care for a being that likes to bite.

Since our three boys already had a real milk producer in Oona, they didn't need KMR. But in our trip to PetSmart during the machete day, when we caught and then released Number Three, I had thrown a couple of cans of the stuff into our shopping cart. One weekend morning, when we were first feeding the family, Matt popped open the KMR and poured some onto a plate as an experiment. Talk about Dr. Jekyll and Mr. Hyde. Oona went crazy for the stuff. Normally she was the epitome of motherly patience (besides the understandable swipe she'd give Number Three now and again). But once the KMR came out, she was transformed. After just one taste of the creamy syrup oozing its way across the blue plastic plate, she hunched up her back, taking up twice as much room over the food and forcing the kittens to bulldoze their way in with their heads. Though Oona didn't quite growl at them, you could tell the way she would turn up the volume of her eating that she was close to it. After that first time, we kept pouring on the KMR, although an eleven-ounce can cost about $10—about what we'd spend to splurge on a can of high-end ground coffee.

That was a good analogy, because the KMR was Oona's morning pick-me-up. It got her up and going and headed out for a day of patrolling, leaving the kittens behind to play and sleep in the backyard. Oona would run across the street to the trees and bushes growing on the Palisades, the steep cliffs that dropped down to the Hudson River, which separated New Jersey from the island of Manhattan. There, she went hunting, often meeting up with her friend Owen, who we thought might be the kittens' father. He was a tomcat, but as we were learning from our research, it wasn't so far-fetched for a father to stick around. Some fathers even bring food to the mother and kittens, defend them by fighting off other cats and raccoons, and take over the parenting duties if the mother dies. If Owen was the dad, he was more an always-on-the-road, Skype-you-from-the-hotel kind, since we never saw him in our yard.

A week after our feline family moved in, I looked out from behind the curtain after breakfast, certain I would see the boys curled up in the back flower bed or running around in circles chasing one another. Only I saw . . . nothing. No small white and black bodies. No paws churning up the dirt. (The entire back bed of ferns, the clouds of white and pink verbena, and the hostas were now officially a dirt pile.)

It took me a minute to realize what I was seeing. The back-yard was empty. There was no place to hide. What you saw of that sixteen-by-seventeen-square-foot space was what you got. Concrete walls on the north and the west sides, a brick patio broken up by just a sliver of dirt where the hostas once thrived, and then a chain-link fence on the north side where a moldy wooden fence used to be until Matt tore it down one weekend because he believed that pressure-treated fences were an insult to all things wooden and authentic.

My first panicked thought was maybe the kittens had gone back next door to Roberto's.

That was when I spotted movement to the right out of the corner of my eye. Through the chain-link fence separating Matt's patio from Lydia and Juan's, I could see Number Three leading a little caravan. The fence hadn't turned out to be a barrier at all. Their heads were still small enough to fit through those little squares. They were bumbling around, nonchalantly checking out Juan and Lydia's concrete patio, painted in gunmetal gray.

I tried some yoga breathing. In through the mouth, out through the nose? Or was it the other way around? Confused, I stopped breathing entirely for a minute and nearly fell over.

My need to control, the guiding principal of my being, kicked into overdrive. I wanted to do something, anything to fix this. But I was thwarted. By three kittens. I couldn't go out there. They knew us, but we had never once tried to pet them or walk toward them. After the Roberto adventure, we were all about letting them chill, getting them used to us just by sight and sound in anticipation of the great snatching that was coming. If I suddenly appeared, putting my tall, mostly hairless, weird-looking self in their domain, they would scatter.

Fine, fine, I thought, if you have to explore, fine, just stay there. Juan and Lydia were on board with our project. Number

Three could keep right on going, marching through the open gate in their wooden fence and into the gated backyard of the neighbor two doors down who had also been notified. Two Spot and Zero trailed behind him, making an uneven little line as they meandered through the fence and were lost to sight.

Right on cue, Matt came in.

"Hey, how are the kittens?" Matt asked as he headed to the stove to pour more coffee.

"Gone, gone," I sputtered. It was all I could manage. Matt, to his credit, waited for me to pull it together. I sat down and explained what had just happened.

Matt laughed, calm as usual.

"They're getting older. It makes sense they're curious. They'll come back when Oona comes home tonight." Seeing my panicked expression, he added, "Or maybe sooner."

"What if they wander off and just disappear and get eaten by a dog on the street?" I asked. It was a legitimate fear. If the neighborhood is cat central, it's Times Square for dogs. Mostly pit bulls, but also feisty Chihuahuas and, now that I was thinking about it, a tough-looking pair of Maltese.

"It can't happen," he explained. "From the roof you can see that the backyards of the houses around us all have wood or concrete fences and solid gates. Until they learn to climb, the farthest they can roam is these four connected yards."

For a while I decided this made sense, but my worry gene was stronger than reason.

"Say they get disoriented and can't figure out how to get back, and die of starvation or thirst?" I asked later in the morning.

"They're just twenty feet away."

That day, I spent a lot of time on top of Matt's house, tracking the kittens' progress from above, creeping surreptitiously from Matt's black roof to Juan's silver one.

Matt was working on his tomatoes in his new roof garden. Matt, it turned out, had discovered a second vocation. Matt loved gardening. Scratch that. He loved tomato gardening. I had never seen such infatuation—especially from someone who a few weeks earlier hadn't known a young tomato plant from a clump of clover. I loved it. I came from a long line of dirt diggers, and to me, earth under the fingernails was one of the most trustworthy signs you could find in another human.

For Matt, it was a miraculous conversion. Soon after discovering the kittens, he set to work on his roof garden. First he hefted up the wood on the ladder through the hole that led to his roof and built a three-foot-by-nine-foot raised bed. Next came the fifty-pound bags of dirt. All systems go, he began planting tomato plant after tomato plant. On visits to his new garden, I kept waiting for him to put in something else to spice it up a little bit with, say, the odd cucumber or pepper. It was tomatoes all the way. Heritage tomatoes from the Greenmarket in New York, each with their own precious story and equally precious price. Hearty, no-nonsense tomatoes from Home Depot. Sad wilting plants saved from near death at the indifferent hands of ShopRite down the hill. Matt couldn't stop himself. His collecting mania now included little pointed-leaf plants.

Watching me step over to Juan's roof from where he was

tending his new crushes, he called in a hushed voice. "Come back. Get off the neighbors' roof!"

I ignored him.

By Sunday evening, I had convinced myself that I didn't need to keep up the reconnaissance from the sky. The boys kept leaving. But they also kept coming back. This was their home. They weren't wandering away yet, just trying out their paws.

The first evening after they walked off, I hadn't believed or accepted this. I had been convinced they had left for good, because I had lost sight of them from the top of the house. I rushed down the stairs, frantic to do something. Matt was at the store, getting more compost for the tomatoes. Having no one to talk me down, I thought about taking the step we never took, getting the key from Juan so I could go into his yard, peek over his fence to see if they were climbing up some far wall, despite what Matt believed, and heading away. I opened the front door, closed it, and opened it again, the sound of the Saturday traffic jostling my nerves even more. I sat down on the bottom step of the stairs and stared at the door. Wouldn't it just be a lot easier to let this go, accept that they had strayed off, that that was the way things were meant to be and that I didn't need to intervene? Didn't I secretly want to go back to the way things had been, Matt visiting me on the week-ends, us not having to make this effort?

I had walked back to the kitchen, turning the possibility of this future over in my mind, absentmindedly pulling back the curtain—and there were the kittens! Two Spot was sitting in a flowerpot of petunias, Zero curled around it like a snake, while Number Three patrolled the perimeter. Heat ricocheted through my body as the tension dropped away. How was it that we always realize how happy and lucky we are, just where we are, in an instant?

Now, a day later in the kitchen, making some pasta for dinner and accustomed to their comings and goings, I peeked outside to see that they were back for the evening. Two Spot and Zero were waiting on the other side of Matt's fence. They were outside. Except they were just sitting there. I noticed Number Three had his head against the chain link. His hind legs dug in, he moved his head back and forth, and suddenly, *pop*, his head went though. That, apparently, was the signal for the other two to stick their own small heads through the gray wire grids, followed by their bodies, emerging as a trio of tiny wandering dominos.

My trio. I went back to the stove, threw some salt in the water, and watched it begin to boil. It may not be possible to learn patience overnight, but I was coming to understand the concept. The past two days had been a hard-learned lesson in forced acceptance. There was nothing I could do as they scampered from yard to yard. I couldn't trap them. I couldn't scold them. I couldn't send Matt out to get lost at Home Depot once more in search of wood to fence them in.

I had to sit there and watch and practice my breathing, which—after talking to my friend, Tevis, who was a yogi of the cool New York partying breed—I remembered was breathe in and out through the nose.

I tossed some penne in the pot and started cutting up tomatoes, mozzarella, and basil. The sharp, tangy smell of the green leaves as I chopped them into short ribbons beneath my knife reminded me of my parents' home in Virginia where, after so many years of wandering, they had settled in, establishing friendships, flower beds, and a vegetable garden where basil was always one of the first plants my father put in the ground in the spring. My childhood up until I was twelve had been the complete opposite. A stream of houses, schools, and companions that changed every time my father was posted to a new air force base. Since I didn't have a say about these wanderings, I learned to exert what little mastery I did have over the situation. I got good at figuring out what other kids liked, erasing parts of myself that didn't mesh, and making up stories to fit in. Here's a classic. After moving to a sprawling development in Fairfax, Virginia, in third grade, I found myself in line next to a very cheerful, very blond girl in my new class named Kimberly, who, out of the blue, told me she liked deer.

"I do, too," I gushed. "I have a deer in my garage."

"A deer?"

"Yes, a fawn, too," I added, upping the ante.

"Could I see them?" she asked, thrilled.

"Not today, but maybe next week," I said, calm in my lies.

She agreed. During that time, we ate lunch together and talked about the deer and what we would feed them when

Kimberly came to my house. I had a great week and didn't feel a twinge of conscience when I told her the day before our play-date that, though they had escaped, she could still come over.

When I got older and still continued to struggle with figuring out what I wanted as opposed to what other people expected of me, I exerted control by working all the time. At *BusinessWeek*, my job, ironically, was to provide analysis. Tricky, since I had little experience in forming my own opinions. I over-reported every single story I wrote. If five interviews might cover it, I did fifteen. I worked hard nailing down every last angle and possible perspective, never realizing that what I needed to know was when to stop, when to trust my own insight. Too much trying to figure out what other people want, too much action, just makes your mind spin, puts you out of control.

That was what I was learning from the kittens. They mattered to me, and I had known enough that I wanted to act on my own to take care of them, without anyone else's encouragement. Inside this experience of choosing for myself, there were pockets of uncertainty that I hadn't anticipated but that I didn't have to master. This was the trick I hadn't understood: choosing didn't guarantee certainty. It just meant being at ease with deciding, with not knowing how it might work out, and being okay with that. Choosing didn't give you control, it gave you freedom.

I drained the pasta then poured it into a bowl with the cheese and tomatoes, drizzling olive oil over it. I felt calm. I was in this moment. I wasn't trying to figure out when to stop, when I had done enough to make this work out. I was at ease with our crazy kittens and their Houdini tricks of popping their too-big heads through chain link. Number Three wanted to explore, but he could be brave because he knew he had a place to come back to. For now, that was all he wanted, the security to try out his choices, to go on an adventure or a misadventure. And I was at ease putting together a simple dinner for me and Matt.

I had to trust this situation, this family of cats. For all their wandering, each night all four still fell asleep in the box out back. I couldn't rein them in just because it made me less anxious. I had to accept. Of course, I couldn't keep it up all the time, but once in a while was a good start.

7

Note to Self:
Kittens Can't Be Counted On

Kitten D-day was set for the morning of July 1. If there was one thing people in our neighborhood looked forward to, it was a party. Holidays were about family, a time to pull everyone closer, and July 4th was a great excuse to do just that. Each house on the block invited their in-laws and cousins, pulled out their grills, piled on the chicken, opened beers, and played music from the start of the day till midnight. Everything was capped off by rousing rounds of bottle rockets, something I was sure would push the kittens into learning how to climb walls.

We decided it made sense to catch the litter before the excitement began. We got up around seven o'clock the morning of the first, nervous but determined. I'd come in on the bus from Manhattan the night before, mentally prepared for a long four-day weekend that was going to be all cats, all the time. The kittens were old enough and Matt and I were both finally at ease with the idea of catching them. But, sure enough, the boys were already off on an early-morning jaunt. Up on the roof, we spotted them in the neighbor's yard two doors down. Luckily, we'd planned for this and had gotten the gate key from Juan, whose house shared the same alleyway.

I waited in front of Matt's house while he brought out the gear: a trap, the blue plastic plate, tins of cat food, a stick, string, tinfoil, a green sheet. Soon there was an odd little pile of hunting paraphernalia on his front stoop. He locked the door and looked up and down the deserted street.

"See anyone?" I asked. It was one thing to be a kitten rescuer with lots of crazy gear. It was another thing for all your neighbors to witness you toting it around.

Matt laughed and shook his head. But he also took another good look around.

Through Matt's class and the reading we had done, one simple mantra had been drilled into us: food is the secret to trapping ferals. It's the only way to get a cat into a cage, and it hardly ever fails. Cats seem to be the masters of the arbitrary, jumping out at your ankles from under the bed when you least expect it. They are, in fact, strict creatures of habit. Once they find the most comfortable spot in the house, whether it's your pillow or that new bowl you just bought for a side table in the hall, they will only give it up under duress.

Cats can't count, but they know time. Start putting out food at a set hour every day, and strays will show up like clockwork. They'll invite their friends and line up outside minutes ahead, watching at the door with scolding looks if you're late. They don't want you wasting their time.

This is why, when it comes to trapping, it's important to set up a feeding routine, something you don't deviate from. Put out bowls of kibble and wet food at, say, seven o'clock every night and eight o'clock every morning for the animals you want to trap, and in a couple of weeks, they'll be hooked. A day or two before your trapping day, you don't feed them. You get them good and hungry, and then you use that empty tummy to get them in the cage.

We learned later that telling most cat people not to feed is a nuclear option. It is inconceivable. They worry about their cats enough as it is, not sleeping out of concern that they're too cold, hot, wet, or thirsty. Now you want them to deprive them of their two daily squares? It makes their minds explode.

But it's rare that trapping will work unless cats are hungry, which is why it's essential. When you do finally arrive with your cage, which you bait with the smelliest food possible (mackerel or tuna in oil being the best options), the hungry cats will waltz into the trap. You'd think the cats would be suspicious of the cages. They're four feet of long, shiny metal. But if there's some appetizing smell hanging in the air, most ferals will give the cage a good sniff over, maybe wander around it a bit, and then head inside for food. They're hungry, remember. And they kind of trust you, or at least they trust that you deliver when it comes to food.

The bait is set at the back of the trap, right behind the trip plate. As the cat walks inside the cage and heads to the food, it steps on the trip plate, causing the gate to slam shut. *Voilà!* You've got yourself a feral cat. Congrats.

Straightforward, right? Most of the time, that's how the trapping goes down. Except, of course, when it comes to kittens. Kittens are a whole other ball game. Their attention spans are as tiny as they are. They may be hungry, but they're just as likely to get distracted by a leaf next to the trap as to remember that, oh yeah, they want to eat.

The other thing to know about our plan was that it was two-pronged. Nothing simple when it came to our litter. We had decided to only catch the kittens first, although we knew we had to get Oona, too, because the prime directive of trapping is catching the mothers. The kittens are cute. They're the emotional connection to this sport. But if you don't trap the mothers and spay them, you're in a losing game. In the Northeast, females can have at least two litters a year. There's no way you're ever going to catch all those kittens and keep up with all that unhampered procreation. The only hope for getting a handle on the feral population, on all the yowling, prowling, dying, and endless litters of kittens who grow up to have litters of their own, is to get the mother.

Some people choose to catch the mother and the kittens in the same go, but not because they plan on holding them together as a happy family. No. Once you decide to catch the cats, you've chosen to separate them. Kittens left with a feral mother just can't be tamed, because they will learn from her, fearing humans and hiding under anything they can find.

If we brought Oona and the kittens in at the same time, it

would mean holding the kittens upstairs in a room we had set aside for them, where we could spend time with them and help tame them. Oona, meantime, would be down in the basement in a cage, while we waited to take her to the vet to have her fixed and then for a couple of days while she recovered. What a nightmare. Kittens and mother meowing back and forth to one another. Matt and I lying in bed, listening to those little pleas to be united, feeling like the great, big, horrible creeps we were.

Our plan, then, was to catch the kittens this weekend and in two weeks, after Oona stopped looking for them, catch her. A trapping marathon was about to commence.

"Wish me luck," Matt said as he lifted up the trap.

At the end of the alleyway, he opened the gate, set down the trap, and stood there for a minute.

Through the open door I saw the kittens. They didn't run, but they were eyeing Matt. They seemed to be reassured by the familiar bright blue food plate.

Matt inched into a sitting position and placed the plate on the ground. For a minute or so, he was alone. Then I saw the kittens creeping toward the meal, led by Number Three as always. He dipped his head down to eat, and the other two followed suit.

Matt surprised me by moving his hand forward and dragging the plate slightly. The kittens backed up a few steps, just watching. They hesitated a moment before inching toward the plate again. After that, each time they started eating, Matt moved the plate. I got it. He was inching the plate toward the cage. Once he got it next to the cage, he started moving it inside. As the kittens became more engrossed in their meal, they seemed to notice each movement less and less to the point where they didn't even balk when the plate went into the cage. They just followed, thinking perhaps that sometimes, plates just move.

The process seemed to last for ages, though it was only minutes. I craned my head to the side, developing a crick in my neck trying to see if they were all inside the trap. Suddenly, *Bam!* The door slammed shut. I jumped, shocked by the finality of the sound. I saw a flurry of white and black movement in the cage. In a flash, Matt reached around to the back of his pants, where he had shoved the green sheet. He unfolded it over the exposed wire cage.

Covering cats up as soon as they're caught is key. It calms them. Ferals that aren't covered will launch themselves against the sides of the cage, the closed door, trying any way they can to get on the other side of the wire, to get back to freedom. A sheet shuts off that hope of escape.

Matt lifted the trap and strode toward me.

That was when I saw Oona, sitting on a concrete ledge right behind Matt, alert and calm. She looked down at the plate of food Matt had left for her and then back up. Patient, noble, completely unsuspecting of what had just happened, she sat waiting for the kittens to come back. Matt's body had blocked her from me, but she must have been there the whole time, watching Matt feed the kittens. She had trusted him with them. She had just sat there and hadn't tried to run him off. I continued staring at her. We were ripping them away from her. I had thought about their separation a great deal. I just never thought I would witness it, never truly felt what it would mean. Kittens grow up, leave their mothers. But cats are social. They tend to stick together even after the litter breaks up, sharing the same territory. In trying to remedy the sad situation they were in because of humans, we humans were making yet one more hard decision for them. Oona would never see her kittens again.

I watched Matt walk toward me, every step sealing a transition that I had wished for so much but that now felt heavy in my hands. He came to a stop in front of me and held up the cage as if in disbelief. I was amazed. We, the most novice of kitten hunters, had managed to pull off our heist. Despite it all, I couldn't help feeling relieved and proud of him.

"We nearly didn't get them all," he said, smiling for the first time. "It was a close call there for a minute." He looked up and down the street. It was 8 A.M., just an hour after we had started. It was the same empty road, but it felt like a different world.

We took them upstairs. As planned, Matt had built an enclosure for them in the front room. The rescuing literature is hectoring on this point: in the beginning, kittens must be kept in an enclosed space, like a cage or a bathroom. It makes them feel safer and forces them to spend time with their new human friends. To hear the training manuals describe kittens and their obsession with small spaces, it seems they would have loved those tin can space capsules from the 1950s.

The bathroom didn't make much sense. I just couldn't

picture the two of us squeezed together, sitting on the tile floor in Matt's tiny bathroom trying to direct small talk at Two Spot huddled behind the toilet. So our ad hoc cage was built into an open closet that didn't have a door. On one side of the closet was a wall, and on the other side Matt had used a staple gun to attach chicken wire to the floor from the opening of the closet to a wall eight feet away. The chicken wire was four feet high, too high for our Lilliputians to jump. Most importantly, the openings in the chicken wire were a lot smaller than the ones in the chain-link fence outside, which had turned Number Three into Houdini. We knew. Matt had lugged the roll of chicken wire outside and compared the size against the chain link one day while the kittens had been off wandering. As a concession to privacy, we'd put a cardboard box in the closet where the kittens could squirrel away. We'd also hung a dark blue sheet from the top of the closet to about two feet off the ground so they could feel hidden even if we were keeping an eye on them all the time.

Matt lowered the trap inside the chicken wire enclosure. He opened one of the doors of the cage, pointed toward the closet, and cautiously stepped back. For a few seconds we waited, muscles tensed, expecting the kittens to shoot out. Then we waited for a minute, muscles relaxed. Then we waited for five minutes, moving from one foot to another, gazing at each other every once in a while.

"I guess they're not coming out," Matt whispered.

"You think?" I replied.

"Maybe we should, you know, encourage them out."

I looked down and considered the trap. All quiet on the kitten front.

"Poke them from behind or something? I'll go get a wooden spoon from downstairs," I replied as I started to move toward the door.

"Wait. Heather. I was thinking more like uncovering the cage."

"Oh. Right. That's another approach."

Matt leaned over and tugged the sheet away bit by bit from the back of the cage, the side that was not open. Zero, Two Spot, and Number Three were huddled on top of one another, pressed against the back wall of the trap. For a minute the little mass of legs and paws and ears was motionless. Then Number Three craned his head up to first gaze at Matt, and then look around. He ducked down quickly.

We waited, expecting them to move toward the part of the cage that was still covered with the sheet, to head toward this dark place to hide themselves, like the cat manuals say they should. The kittens, though, didn't seem to have read the same handbook. They stayed in place.

"Maybe we should cover them up and leave them until they come out on their own?" I said.

"Yeah." Matt nodded.

As he reached over to pull the sheet back onto the trap, Number Three glanced up at him again and, with a huge stretch forward of his front legs, bounded out of the cage, ricocheting against the wall of the cardboard box in the closet, before running around to the entrance and hiding inside. Two Spot and Zero, abandoned by their braver brother, both stood up and rushed after him. A minute later, the entire room was quiet, the only movement the slight swaying of the sheet.

"I guess they changed their minds," Matt said.

We tiptoed out of the room.

A n hour was all I could handle. I went upstairs and, cracking the door open, shuffled toward the cage. They weren't out in the enclosure. After hesitating a minute I couldn't help myself. I tugged the sheet to the side.

The closet was empty.

"Matt!" I yelled. "They're gone."

He was up in the stairs in two seconds.

"They can't be," he said in disbelief, checking inside the closet.

We just looked at each other for a minute.

"They have to be here someplace. The door was closed the whole time."

"But if they aren't in there, where are they? Maybe they found a hole in the wall somewhere? Maybe we have cats in our walls?"

Matt just stared at me. Oh right, they didn't need to scratch their way through plaster to find a small place to creep into. This room was all Matt, and that made it kitty-hiding heaven. Boxes upon boxes of books with plenty of places to hide between and behind lined the sides. An old futon slumped against the wall. Shelving units full of magazines and files. They could be anywhere.

Matt and I started doing reconnaissance, searching the other closet, craning to see if they were hiding between the stacks of pictures, leaning up against one another on the floor, or behind a pile of shoes.

"Why can't we find them?"

"They're small and they're well trained," he reminded me.

Finally, Matt started checking the cracks between the heavy metal filing cabinets that he collected off the street on the Lower East Side. He had a row of five, all lined up next to one another.

"Aha," he muttered.

I walked over and leaned down. There they were, in a two-inch space between the last cabinet and the wall. They were stacked one on top of the other so that all we could see was a pile of tiny kitten heads and front paws. Number Three was on the bottom, so he must have been the first to find the crack, and then Two Spot and Zero must have thrown themselves in on top of him. They were a living furry totem pole.

"How did you guys manage that?" I asked them.

We tried to pry them out with a broom handle, but they didn't budge. They were good and stuck. So we decided the only option was to take all the shelves out of the cabinet next to them so that we could move it a little to the left and get the kittens unstuck.

The last part of the maneuver was tricky. With the drawers out, the cabinets were pretty light. But Matt had to reach inside one opening, lift the cabinet up from the inside, and swing it ever so slowly toward himself to avoid squashing the kittens. I kneeled in front of the opening with a pillowcase, prepared to grab the little fellows.

"Ready?" Matt said from above.

"This is crazy."

"No, seriously, ready?"

"All right. Okay."

"One, two . . . three."

The cabinet moved. The kittens dropped down. I reached in, grabbed Zero, shoved him in the bag, grabbed Two Spot, shoved him in the bag, and then, just as Number Three looked like he was about to get his wits, I nabbed him.

"Keep them in the sack for right now," Matt told me.

He left the room and came back a few minutes later with more sheets. I watched, bemused, as he lay the sheets over the chicken wire, covering it over and closing up all the holes they must have used as footholds to climb to freedom.

"They got through somehow," he explained as he worked.

I deposited the pillowcase on the other side of their cage. They shot out like rockets. When we checked on them half an hour later, they were still there. We had caught our kittens—twice in one day.

It didn't take me long to start feeling guilty. Less than twenty-four hours, in fact. My eyes barely cracked open the next morning before my brain went into overdrive, spitting out a list of things to feel responsible for.

I felt bad about breaking up their cat family unit. About shutting them off from the familiar sounds, sights, and smells that had surrounded them since birth. About encasing them in walls and floors and ceilings, in an environment they didn't know. About subjecting them to our old air conditioner, which sounded like a buzz saw.

I felt awful about everything I could think of—even birds, I realized, as I looked out the window at the overgrown forsythia bush that hung over from the neighbor's backyard into Matt's. A group of sparrows was sitting in the leaves, hopping lightly from branch to branch, noisily encouraging a baby as it learned to fly. Zero, Number Three, and Two Spot would probably end up in an apartment and never hunt again. That's where my guilt stopped, because even I couldn't keep that thread going. Eating birds was awful because of the devastation to the bird population. I was 100 percent for keeping cats indoors. So I felt good about bird deprivation.

I reached back and adjusted my pillows, not ready to face the day.

The source of my angst was the fact that now that we had the kittens, we had to launch Phase Two of our plan: socialization. Socialization is a grand word for taming the wild beast that is a kitten. It comes down to not getting your eyes slashed out. Despite their adorable round eyes and tiny paws, our kittens were wild. Bringing them inside, giving them some peace and quiet . . . that was not going to transform these feral animals into something cute and cuddly.

We had to foist ourselves on Number Three, Two Spot, and

Zero so that they got used to us. We needed to spend a lot of time with them, talking to them, petting them, eventually even picking them up. That would make the kittens, taught from birth to hide, scared out of their wits. They were going to hate every minute of it.

I was coming face-to-face with their fear. I knew it would get worse. I was being forced to wonder whether, if an animal was well fed but clearly scared to death whenever it saw you, it was better off outside.

I was the responsible party, the pushy, let's-get-this-done-now, I-know-what's-best-for-the-kittens one. As someone who worked hard most of her life to not take a stand on things that seemed to count, this new position was ridiculous. I had rarely gone out and gotten what I wanted in the world. I had avoided it to such a point that I had never known what I wanted. Instead, I had gone about accomplishing what other people expected from me. It's not as if someone ever told me that this was what I needed to do in order to achieve success, it's just that, after so many years of moving around as a child, I got good at defining myself by the expectations of people around me. I never gave myself freedom to try out other ideas and potential futures before I locked into the trajectory I decided I wanted for myself. So, if after choosing to be a reporter, working for one of the top maga- zines in New York City was considered to be the definition of success by most people around me, that's what I accepted as the thing I should aim to do for myself. And if working all the time was what everyone in New York did, I threw myself into that as a definition of success.

Many people were comfortable marching forward through life, certain in themselves and their ability to judge the right thing for them to do, or at least certain of being able to handle the fallout. Other people had an idea of who they were, confident in their sense of themselves and their ability to adapt to failure. I never did. I watched those people all my life, amazed, admiring, bemused. I never quite understood how a person could be so sure in the knowledge that they truly know what they are doing—or so willing to accept the consequences of being wrong.

The classic example was the string of promising (or maybe not, I don't know, I never got close enough) boyfriends over the years. Christopher, Jasper, Peter. Whatever flavor they came in, French, German, American, it didn't matter. Neither did my age, whether in high school, college, or work. They showed interest. I was attracted. Then, one or two months in, I couldn't handle the responsibility of a relationship, of their feelings, of mine. Each time, I pulled the plug as soon as it got serious.

Now, I was doing what I had never been able to: accepting that a choice I wanted to make was going to impact not just myself but another being, plans were going to succeed and fail. *Because of me.* For so long, I had believed that letting things happen around me meant I was off the hook in terms of responsibility. I would exert just enough control over tiny, useless aspects of things to make myself feel comfortable, but, distracted by minutiae, I passively allowed outside forces to dictate my moves. But lo and behold, it turned out that not making a choice was still a choice. Who knew? Not me, at least not for thirtysomething years. The realization I was facing now with the task of taming these wild kittens before me was that it might just be better to strike out and form the moment, rather than turning away and having it mold you.

Every time after I broke up with one of those men, I pined for months, working with an obsessive yet still indirect fervor to get them back, hanging around at the same cafés, parties, libraries. In high school, I stuffed cards in a onetime boyfriend's mailbox late at night, a particular favorite being one featuring an elephant about to jump into a tiny bucket filled with water and the caption *No Guts, No Glory*. Romantic, right? No surprise then that these belated campaigns never worked. Instead of shaping a healthy relationship, I had let my fear of being the keeper of someone else's emotions enshroud me in unhappiness and paralyze me to the point of helplessness.

With the kittens, if we decided not to act, they would grow up feral, sure to get into fights over territory with other tomcats, be hungry, exist in fear of making it through the winter or even across the street, lucky to live another four years. That is a huge consequence to come from doing nothing.

Yet, what if I screwed up? What if being proactive and attempting to shape a situation went wrong? Who could I blame then? Would I be able to ever make another attempt so contrary to my nature again? Would the drama I was putting the kittens through be worse than leaving them in the life that every other feral lived? Because while I was pretty sure that cat therapists existed (this was, after all, the New York area), I doubted they did pro bono work for wild kittens—from New Jersey, for goodness' sake. I rolled back over on my side and tugged the covers over my head.

An hour later, having managed to pull myself out of bed, I was headed to the bathroom when I heard soft noises coming down the hall. There was a little *chirrup* answered by a *chirp* punctuated by a sprinting of feet. A distinctive *trill* and a sort of *chewp*, another *chirrup*, finished off by a *thunk* and a loud *mewl*.

It sounded as if a flock of clumsy chickens had settled in behind the door.

They were the sweetest, silliest sounds possible, ones that reminded me of my nephew when he was two, walking around defying gravity, babbling to himself and his scarlet red stuffed bear, Biff. But baby chicks hadn't appeared as if by magic. The kittens, toddlers, too, with their short attention spans and bumbling gaits, were chirruping to one another as they wandered around their new home.

Chirp! "*See how I can hang on this curtain with just my claws!*"

Trill! "*Wow, I can do that, too!*" *Thunk. Chewp.* "*I mean . . . I could do that.*"

Gallop, gallop, chirrup! "*Look at me jump!*"

Trill! "*I see a fly!*"

Trill, trill, trill! "*Where? Where? Where?*"

Mewl. "*Oops. False alarm.*"

Another thought occurred to me. Maybe they weren't romping around in play. Maybe these chirrups spelled revolution.

Perhaps one of the kittens (bets were always on Number Three) had scaled the curtain wall and was running loose again in the room, relaying signals to his brothers about all the great hiding places he was discovering.

Trill! "Those hairless creatures will never find us in this hole under the floor!"

I was about to burst in, but I had learned a thing or two recently about cats and what they thought about fast movements. Instead, I cracked the door, poked my head around, and scanned the room. No kitten legs running free, no flash of fur as a baby catapulted itself into some dark spot. But also no more chirping. I inched into the room, careful to close the door behind me, and then tiptoed over to the kittens' cage. The open enclosure was empty. I pulled the curtain back, and there they were, one, two, three small bodies squeezed together in the cardboard box. Zero's head and tail were buried between his brothers' bodies, so all I saw was a round white tummy. But Number Three and Two Spot looked up, two pairs of enormous eyes studying me, curious despite themselves. Number Three, sitting there so still, wasn't his cocky self, but did he look just a bit annoyed at being interrupted? Two Spot was warier. His huge ears, perked up and toward me, were on high alert.

Watchful. But they weren't quivering balls of fur anymore.

Maybe the chirping meant what it sounded like and I didn't need to search so hard for another answer. Perhaps it was happiness after all.

I looked around. The kittens did have the best room in the house. With four windows lining the eastern side of the room, a high ceiling, and clean white walls, the space was buoyed by light. Through the glass, the leaves from the trees across the street swayed slightly in the heat. Even that buzzing air conditioner was quieter than the noises outside, the blaring car alarms, the piercing sirens of the fire station one block away, the revving of the motorcycles that raced up the hill in front of Matt's house.

I hadn't managed to make everything perfect for them from the get-go. Some things were going to be scary, at least in the short term. Some things were tragic, like being separated forever from Oona.

Not everything was wrong. There were still the things they could chirp about behind the closed door. Perhaps I was on the right track. I deserved a good cup of coffee.

8

Above All, Protect Your Eyes

Walking through the door later that morning, back from my weekly Sunday *Times* run, I almost plowed into Matt. He was standing at the bottom of the stairs juggling a couple of plastic plates, two jars of baby food, and a few little tins of wet kitten food.

"Hi," he said, smiling brightly as he turned to walk upstairs.

His excitement and eagerness to get cracking with the kittens was fun to see.

"Hey," I replied as I followed him. He walked into the kittens' room. Handing the supplies to me, he proceeded to sling one leg and then the other over the side of the fence.

"What's on the agenda?" I asked.

"A little animal taming," he replied, as though he spent every weekend socializing kittens. He reached out for the food and plates and sat down in front of the closet.

This was what I loved about Matt. I leaned against the wall and settled in to watch. This was what had made me think a month ago, without questioning the impulse, that we could save these kittens. It wasn't that Matt was one of those fearless people who doesn't contemplate the consequences of things. He and I were alike in our tendency to sit and study situations through. But Matt didn't let the considerations bog him down. He thinks through possible outcomes and moves forward. If things didn't work out as hoped, that's just one potential result. It doesn't mean everything is a failure, just that it's time to move to the next thing.

When Matt and I first started dating, I had still been following my instinct to eject him as a potential boyfriend at any excuse.

"He's too quiet," I said to Gail, the friend who had set us up at her party in Harlem.

"Give him a chance," Gail replied. "He's thoughtful. He's a keeper."

"He can't seem to make decisions," I complained to my therapist, Susan.

"You mean because he asks you where you want to go out for dinner?" she joked back.

"I don't like his shoes. They're kind of goofy," I told my mother, describing some old boxy sandals he liked to wear.

"You're kidding me," she replied.

I was right about the goofy part, just not the cowardly fleeing instinct behind that comment. He did collect odd things, from old canvas camp beds to metal electric fans from the 1930s. But I was glad I managed to make it through those early two months, overcoming my urge to sabotage us. Because it brought me to this point: to the realization that not many of my past boyfriends would overcome their initial resistance to rescuing cats the way Matt had, simply because he understood it meant so much to me. Now, here he was, my kitten tamer.

Matt held in his hand a jar we hoped would be the secret to socializing. The magical properties of Gerber chicken baby food are real and potent. Kittens are true to their feline caste. You can't tame a cat. It has to choose to be domesticated. The only way to convince a feral kitten that it should come anywhere near a human is through treats. We had read in our cat guides that Gerber baby mush is the most irresistible food of any food known to felines. Gerber turkey will do in a pinch, but with chicken you're guaranteed success. It is kitten kryptonite.

Yet like all truly powerful weapons, chicken baby food must be used with care.

We had laid the groundwork, as we had been instructed. During the first two days after we caught the boys, we put out plates of wet food and KMR all the time, leaving them alone to eat. The idea was to get them used to eating here and to make sure they weren't sick. We had wondered if they would eat in this new, unfamiliar environment, without their mother to lead the way, but we didn't need to worry. Each time we put a plate of food into the enclosure and came back an hour later, it was licked clean. On the first day, Matt stayed in the room at a distance to watch them all eat, just to make sure that Number Three wasn't skewing the results and chowing down on all of the food. They seemed healthy and weren't refusing food, which was the groundwork we needed. It meant we could safely move on to step two: deploying food as bait to begin socializing them.

Now the real work began. We had to start using the kibble to make them come out and spend time with us. Thus, the kitty kryptonite. Regular wet food made our boys happy, but they had never been exposed to the remarkable power of Gerber. We had held it in reserve, knowing its time would come.

Matt opened up the baby food, waving the stubby jar around so that the kittens could get the full effect of the pungent sweet smell. Then he dolloped the contents of one jar, and then another, onto the plate, lowered it to the ground, moved to the back of the enclosure, and sat down to wait. By leaving the chicken baby food near the door, Matt was making the temptation to investigate irresistible. But it wasn't a freebie. The trade-off was they had to eat while he was in the enclosure. The idea was to associate our presence with this delicious substance so that, little by little, they would become happy to see us and we could tame them. Sounded promising, but according to our reading, the whole process could take weeks. Every action we took for granted with tame kittens—being held, purring when caressed, even playing with a toy—was something we had to teach our boys. The amazing thing would be if this whole ploy worked out. Looking at Matt sitting on the floor of the empty enclosure, it was hard to imagine. Matt was, after all, just one person up against our three kittens.

Fifteen minutes into this standoff, I decided that a better idea was to cede the battlefield for the moment and get reinforcements in the guise of a sandwich.

I only heard about the miraculous event after the fact. Suffice it to say, the combination of baby mush and this particular man proved too much for the kittens. At least for Number Three.

Number Three. He could never help himself. His curiosity, his bravado, and his nose got the best of him in most situations.

Matt sat for forty-five minutes. His legs started falling asleep. He studied the blue sheet, a crack he hadn't noticed in the ceiling, the far wall. He ended up reading the pieces of the articles from the pieces of newspaper laid on top of one another on the floor. It was haiku reading, with just a few sentences about the booming real estate market in Manhattan bleeding into a story about artisanal pickles in Brooklyn and a review of a new off-Broadway play. He was so fixated on trying to piece together pieces of the pickle story that he nearly missed Number Three's appearance.

The sound of quiet, tentative licking turning into gulping alerted Matt to a change in the situation.

Figuring out how to *move* around kittens is a science. You can move, but only in increments that the cat was convinced couldn't develop into a lunge. Lunges precipitate cat warfare. So they've become masters at conveying a lot by how slowly they move. (Though a correlating belief they seem to hold—that they become

invisible if they change position very, very slowly—just baffles me.)
However, when in Rome, move incredibly slowly, like you're a cat
swimming through molasses.

Matt tilted his head up from the picture of the Brooklyn
pickle maker, craning his chin up bit by bit until his face was
level. He was watching Number Three devour the two jars of
baby food that he doled out on the blue plate.

Number Three was a champion eater. Cats tend to be delicate even when they are feeding. A very hungry cat will sort of
bury its face into a good plate of food and chow down, growling
even. But on the whole, cats mainly tend to be dignified.

Not Number Three. Number Three gobbled so much food
that he had developed a habit of putting his white paw on the
plate to keep it from scooting out from underneath him. His jaw
seemed to have this ability to unhinge, like a snake's, so he could
get even more food down his throat.

That was how Number Three ate when it came to his regular
food. Now that he had tasted Gerber nirvana, his eating sped
up. Within a matter of a few minutes, a heaping serving of yellow
baby mush had disappeared inside Number Three.

The plate empty, Number Three collapsed in happiness. His
stomach was full of the best, creamiest, most satisfying goop he
had ever had, outside of some good mother's milk. It was time,
naturally, to do a little bathing. Number Three lifted his right
paw to his mouth, wet it with his tongue, and started swiping it
across his face. He repeated the movement a few times but was
so full that just the slight push of his limb made him plop over.

That was when Number Three realized he wasn't alone. Lying on his side, he noticed Matt for the first time.

Matt hadn't moved an inch, though his sleeping legs were now officially not a part of his body. All he had adjusted was the angle of his head. When Number Three noticed Matt, Matt was looking right at him.

Looking directly into a cat's eyes is the last thing you want to do when a feline first notices you. Most cats, especially feral ones, see eye contact as a sign of aggression. They make decisions about their environment based on staring. They fight based on who is staring at who. Wild kittens especially hate direct eye contact, we had read.

Not our Number Three. After his initial movement of surprise, he was just curious to see Matt sitting there. He cocked his head a little to the side, his paw still hanging up in the air in mid–cleaning swipe. He stared back at Matt. Matt dropped his gaze, the way he had read in the book, and looked back at Number Three, expecting him to be gone or to have also dropped his eyes down. Nope, the tiny bugger was still gazing right at him.

It was almost as though Number Three had put it together. Amazing food just appeared, and so did that weird hairless fellow in front of him. Did he have any more? Number Three went back to bathing. Oona had taught the kittens well. They were obsessive bathers just like their mom and had immaculate white and black coats.

For the next ten minutes, Matt didn't stir. Number Three finally managed to heave his bloated stomach up along with the rest of his body and totter under the curtain into the box with his brothers. Matt propelled his tingling legs up and out of the room without falling. He came downstairs, sat next to me on the couch where I was reading the paper, and gave me a big, triumphant kiss.

"It's going to work," he said and smiled.

At least it was going to work on Two Spot and Number Three. Baby food was a revelation in many ways, not all good. Within two days, we realized we had a grave problem on our hands. By withholding food except whenever we were sitting at the back of the enclosure, we did force Two Spot and Number Three to come out three times a day. But Zero didn't eat for forty-eight hours straight. That had us worried because Zero had a history of being sickly at times.

When I first saw Zero, he was a stocky little fellow, a prize-fighter who swung his white shoulders back and forth when he walked. Yet, about a week before we caught the kittens, he had started looking lethargic and listless, huddling up close to Oona at every opportunity. Instead of running to the food like the others, he would amble over, taste the kibble with just the tip of his tongue, and slide back on his hind legs. We were torn about catching him before we trapped the other kittens. It might be more stressful to bring him in and hold him alone than to let him stay outside a little longer. It was just a week of waiting, after all. After two days of watching and worrying, tracking his slow movements, how he ate just tiny bites at mealtimes, we decided over emails traded between us at work that if he still looked sick when we fed them that night, we'd act. The problem was, when Matt got home, he couldn't find the net he was sure was somewhere in the basement. So instead, he crafted one out of a bent wire hanger, some duct tape, and cheesecloth. Looking at Matt, clutching the drooping makeshift contraption in his right hand, made me feel even more uncertain about our plan.

We put out a dinner plate of dry and wet kitten food and waited, kneeling across from each other on the hard linoleum squares beside the sliding glass door and watching as the cats came up to eat. Matt clutched the makeshift net tightly in his right hand.

Two Spot and Number Three hunched over the blue plastic plate of food, gobbling up big bites. Zero just sat back on his hind legs, watching them, his head drooping slightly.

"Should I do it?" Matt whispered, looking at me across the darkened room.

He was close enough, and Zero was slow enough these days.

"I don't know," I whispered back. "Maybe we should just go ahead and catch all three."

"I'm not even sure this net will hold one," Matt replied.

"If we catch him and he gets loose in the house, we'll really be in a pickle."

We both sat in silence in the dark, gazing at each other, unable to make a decision.

"Wait, he's starting to move," Matt said in a frantic tone.

I looked back to the kittens, and sure enough, Two Spot and Number Three had finished eating and were ambling away. I saw Matt move the net slightly. He's going to do it, I thought. But before he could bring it down, Zero had turned to follow, moving fast for the first time in days. We'd missed our chance. The next morning, maybe sensing a hint of what we planned in the air, Zero started eating a little better. Relieved, we figured he was on the road to mending.

Now that he was inside, he'd stopped eating yet again and was looking more listless by the day.

"Oh gosh, what do we do?" I said. Matt and I were huddled outside the kittens' door, talking in quiet tones like we were in the hallway of a hospital.

"Let's take them all to the vet tomorrow," Matt replied without a pause.

"I can't do that," I replied. "I have a very big interview scheduled."

My interview had taken weeks to schedule. I couldn't cancel it. Then there was just the hassle of the Lincoln Tunnel, wrangling their little bodies into a carrier, navigating parking.

"I can take them," said Matt, breaking in on my little bubble of worry.

I looked up from where I'd been studying the scuffed-up floor. I had forgotten there were two of us involved. I didn't have to do everything. He smiled.

The next morning, sporting a few scratches on his hands, Matt whisked them into New York to the Cat Practice. Around noon, walking across Park Avenue after my interview, I got a call from him.

"Zero is sick, but he'll be fine," Matt launched in right away.

"He has ulcers on his tongue. Dr. Sheheri thinks he might have a viral infection. The ulcers make it uncomfortable for him to eat."

"What did she say to do?"

"He's not dehydrated at this point and seems mostly okay. She says we just need to watch Zero. He should be able to fight the virus."

"That's wonderful," I babbled, relieved. It was beautiful outside. Our little prizefighter would be okay. We hadn't waited too long. "Oh, wait, I'm getting another call. I have to take this." Just as I was about to hang up, I shouted into the phone with all the relief I was feeling: "You're amazing!" I heard a laugh as I clicked over to the other call. Like that, I was back in work mode, chatting with the creator of *Rocketboom*, the Internet's hottest video podcast (for that second). He was in the middle of an unexpected and messy breakup with Amanda, the show's popular and equally hot host. The Internet was all agog, and I had to get back to the office and write up something fast.

Later, after posting my oh-so-important momentary exclusive about the latest Web brouhaha, I got to settle into my chair and read about something that was important only to me. I clicked on the email Matt had sent with his full report.

"So everyone is fine," he wrote at the end of a rundown about fleas and shots that I found riveting. "They got poked probed and swabbed more than anything. handled by at least two doctors, and four technicians, and me. cooed over by two receptionists. hissed at by one big cat. lots of loud traffic noise. horrified by the whole experience, but hopefully they'll get over it."

They did. Within a few days, Zero had turned the corner

and was back to being as healthy and stubbornly aloof as ever. He was adorable.

Kitten taming forced me to do something I'd been avoiding even thinking about recently: spending the week, and not just weekends, at Matt's. For two years, I'd managed to dodge this seemingly inevitable fate. He'd asked a couple of times in the beginning if I wanted to stay over Sunday night and commute with him on Monday. I could tell he thought it would be cute, heading out in the morning as a couple, but I just kept coming up with an endless variety of early-morning meetings that I had to attend, and after a while, he stopped mentioning it. Either he was onto me or he came to the conclusion that every single person in the tech world was programmed to meet at eight on Monday mornings. For me, my weekend-only visits were much more meaningful, like little breaks from my real life. Going home on my own, being in my place all week, working crazy hours meant I was still an independent New Yorker. Those weekends in Union City with Matt, and now the kittens, had remained separate somehow.

I'd seen a change coming as we'd advanced down the path to kitten rescue. But I'd tried not to think about it. As long as I didn't think about it too much and kept repeating to myself that it was only temporary, arriving at Matt's place after work each day was sort of a lark. After all, unlike me, he had cable TV.

Once Matt explained the remote control to me half a dozen times, I could even sometimes watch it.

I also had the kittens as entertainment. That's to say, Two Spot and Number Three. Zero just turned his back on me and wedged himself into whatever corner he could find. The two braver brothers were a different story. They were curious, and they loved the baby food—both two good developments in our favor.

How I wish I'd discovered three ten-minute YouTube videos entitled "Tough Love" before my bumbling began. These online clips, with a sweet piano and xylophone score, are narrated by Mike Phillips. Mike, tall, thin, with a sharp-planed face and cultured voice straight out of a 1940s black-and-white Hollywood screwball caper, was a cat rescuers' cat rescuer. Living in Chelsea in the late 1990s, Mike was a pioneer of New York's trapping community. He cofounded the Urban Cat League, a group that fixed and fed ferals, and spearheaded turning an abandoned lot into a feline sanctuary where local cat caregivers worked together to take care of former strays, tame kittens, and find homes for the cats.

"Tough Love" opened with Mike, camping headlamp strapped to his forehead, thick leather gloves up to his elbows, entering a crawl space under an apartment building to catch three minuscule kittens. The next part of the film, after he'd caught the litter and installed them in a giant dog crate in the cat sanctuary, was a socialization tutorial that started with a segment entitled "Panic." That was exactly what most untamed kittens did at first. Mike, though, never did. In these videos, which a few years later I would watch for hours on a loop, he demonstrated the slow and steady steps needed for taming a wild kitten. You started with getting them used to eating near you, then to eating from your finger, letting you pet them, getting them to eat in your lap, and finally letting you hold them. Through asides such as "You work in increments, one inch at a time"; "The goal of feeding by hand is to overcome the kittens' fear of hands coming at them and human contact"; and "Every inch is very difficult to accomplish," Mike unveiled the magic behind taming wild babies.

What Mike demonstrated was that you cannot hurry kittens along. You can't create a timetable and expect them to sign up. Slow, steady, and Zen. These are the only approaches that will work—as long as you're armed with food. Everything you know about domesticated cats—that they want to sit on your computer keyboard, sleep on your head, demand to be petted just so— applies not at all to an untamed kitten. Feral babies don't care a fig about you. What they want most in the world is to get away from you. You have to go at their pace and give them the space to learn to trust you.

Patience is the main virtue you need when taming a cat.

This was unfortunate, because I didn't have any. It wasn't just the boys who were in training. It was also me.

I did a lot of sitting during that first week. After my commute from the city, I'd change out of my work clothes and climb into the enclosure bearing a plate of food, Two Spot and Number Three waiting in the back of the closet for me to settle down along the edge of the enclosure. They would then inch slowly toward the plate, eyeing me each step of the way as if I was going to swoop down and grab them at any minute. Which I would have done in a second if I could have. It was killing me that I couldn't pet them. Kittens are cute in general, with their pudgy tummies, round, wide eyes, and stubby tails. Ours were impossibly adorable. Their fur was so white and downy, their little whiskers long and soft. After all the waiting and the planning, the plotting and scheming, they were here with us, within just a hand's reach. But I couldn't pet them. I couldn't rub their ridiculously huge ears. I couldn't pick them up and cuddle them the way you do with every other kitten in the world. Because they were wild. They had to learn to trust me. I had to let our boys just get used to eating near me. Small steps, I had to remind myself each time I got near them. Stupid small steps.

So, the kittens would eat. I would sit there. They would give themselves a bath. I would sit there. They would start walking along the edge of the enclosure as long as I would sit there. I imagined that, late one night, they'd had a short discussion among themselves and decided to pretend I didn't exist as long as I went along with the notion. I had grudgingly agreed to this détente only because I had many other secret plans of my own mapped out for the weeks to come. Patience. Whatever.

In the short term, it helped our mutual Kabuki play of ignore-the-other-being that Matt had added a plant and a balancing bar made out of four pieces of wood to the enclosure. This gave the kittens something to pay attention to other than the human trying to pretend she wasn't there. Two Spot was always more skittish, the one that would jump straight up in the air and disappear into the closet when I so much as moved my hand. But in no time he'd bonded with the spider plant. Two Spot loved lying on his side, curling his body about the ceramic pot, and then pushing his hind legs to propel himself in wild circles around it. When he wasn't doing endless circuits, he was resting like a lion cub on top of the pot. Soon, the plant didn't resemble a living organism as much as a container with green stringy bits straggling over the side. While Two Spot wooed his poor little plant, Number Three would wander around the enclosure, looking for trouble and springing onto the corners of the newspaper that stuck up. Number Three got a lot of pleasure out of annoying his two siblings. He would scramble up onto the climbing bar and swat down at whoever tried to climb up after him, running from one end to the other on the piece of wood in glee. He would lie near the bottom of the sheet that hung in front of the closet and tackle anyone who tried to get by him. He thudded up and down the enclosure, thundering past Two Spot on his ceramic planter.

Number Three got so much joy out of these escapades that one morning, as he crashed by Two Spot, his speed ricocheted him across the enclosure and right into my lap, ending up in an upside-down heap of legs. We were both shocked for a second, staring into each other's eyes. His fur was warm and thistledown soft against my legs. I could almost feel his tiny heart thumping as his minuscule rib cage went up and down and he caught his breath from his tumble. I smiled because that was what you did when a tiny baby fell when it was playing. I reached down to straighten out the warm, furry baby splayed across my legs.

Wrong move. The sight of my hands moving toward him freaked him out. His eyes became massive round circles, his head jerked back, and his claws came out. Number Three turned with a clumsy motion and launched himself over my knees, grabbing for whatever hold he could find. He scrambled to the closet and hunkered down.

Kitten claws may be tiny, but to compensate for their size, they're sharp. I had made two rookie mistakes. I had tried to treat him as if he were tame. And I'd worn shorts. My knee burst into a hot, throbbing point of pain. The top of my left knee started bubbling red, oozing through the thin scratches Number Three had left. I stared down, concentrating on the blood. Because the one thing I knew was that I couldn't jump up, I couldn't yell, I couldn't scare the kittens. Instead, I defaulted to my yoga breathing, which I found myself using quite a lot these days, and pulled my mouth into a pained smile. During the brief ruckus, Two Spot had dropped behind his plant. Peeking around the side, he stared at the weirdly grinning human across from him. I tightened my jaw even more. I had ridden and fallen off a lot of horses when I was young. Getting back into the saddle was the key to erasing bad memories.

"Who wants some baby food?" I managed to eke out. Reaching to the side where I had one jar left, I twisted the lid. The seal broke with a pop, and Number Three's head emerged from behind the curtain like a jack-in-the-box. I managed to spoon out the contents to him and Two Spot, moving a yellow spoon back and forth between their little tongues. Calm restored, I hoisted myself up with effort, climbed over the sheet-draped chicken wire, and hobbled out of the room. The searing pain from my throbbing skin reinforced the lesson I had just learned: never touch a wild kitten until he is ready. There were reasons to be patient, with pain and blood both figuring high up on the list.

Part of why I was so eager to get on to the petting the kittens stage of the game was I thought that touching would mean that we were taming them; it would signal that they were on their way to liking us. Doesn't petting mean caring? Doesn't accepting a caress mean returned affection? When would we have proof that we were making real progress?

The bloody knee incident didn't have any lasting consequences. The kittens were still willing to come out and eat while we were around. In fact, within three days, we were able to sit next to the plate while they had their meals, ending our banishment to the other side of the enclosure. What was more, we could move around a little without causing all three to bolt into the closet. This was huge progress, especially the moving bit. Because two or three daily sessions during which our legs fell asleep each time was not an experience we were eager to continue. We would spend an hour or two each morning and each evening, before and after work, socializing the kittens. The dead weight, painful tingling, and sense that you're about to tumble over onto a trio of babies is disconcerting.

So. Movement and proximity opened up new worlds. One evening, I sat cross-legged on the ground next to the kittens as they munched their dinner. Two Spot nudged Number Three slightly, forcing him to move to his left. Number Three realized as he shifted position that the baby jar was sitting open next to me. What he didn't realize was that my hand was resting on the floor next to the container. I had been waiting for just such an opening. As Number Three pushed by me to nudge his nose into the glass jar, I lifted my hand slightly and touched his fur. It was the lightest movement, just a sweep across his back before he stepped quickly back, shocked enough at the touch to give up the baby food and return to eating at the plate with his brothers. But that was all. He hadn't run away to hide. I had finally done it! I had been able to touch one of our wild trio. He'd retreated, but I'd expected that, and I'd dreaded that he'd actually disappear. Instead, there he was, a little wary, but willing to stay out in the open. With me.

After that, I became an expert at sneak petting. I waited until Number Three and Two Spot were engrossed in eating and would brush their heads, sides, and backs. Zero, clever as always, made sure to keep to the far side of the plate, so I decided to be happy with the fact that he was at least coming out and focus first on the other two. Maybe, if he saw that it wasn't such an awful thing, he'd come around. Because when it came to petting, I didn't linger. I would just brush along their soft baby fur with the lightest touch. But each time I ran two fingers down their spine, they hunched down or moved to the right or the left, throwing annoyed and scared glances at me, instantly aware they'd been touched. But they also knew they had the freedom to retreat and then come back to eating. I wasn't punishing them by removing food, I was just bothering them while they ate.

That was the thing, though. They didn't like any of this. I *was* bothering them, and they would have been much happier if I hadn't insisted on all this petting. They put up with it because I didn't try to hold them in place, because they could dodge their bodies out of the way for a minute and then get back to the business of eating. They were young kittens with hours of playing to do, so they needed lots of nourishment. Caressing them was like trying to touch a patch of tall flowers nodding in the wind. They would bob and weave their heads and bodies, not enjoying my touch but accepting it for the sake of baby food.

Still, there was something magical happening here, a transformation that even I, impatient as I was, had to admit was incredible. We were forming a bond, however new and fragile and reliant on baby food. They had an understanding based on their knowledge of how I moved and how my voice sounded, and I learned to be sensitive to their quick jerks away, ear twitches, and wary recognition. They weren't any more attached to me than before—I represented food to them, not pleasure and not company—but they accepted that I was around to stay. This wasn't exactly what I was hoping for. But it was something I could work with. We were four beings learning to know one another, to allow for mistakes, to adjust our expectations. We were beginning to trust in the moment and in one another. That was enough to start with.

9

Old Demons

Matt might live a mile from New York as the crow flies, but I was not a bird. I was now a tristate rush-hour day commuter with all the pleasure that entails. Racewalking through Times Square to the bus station, dodging the clumps of tourists wandering under the blinking, shiny lights of 42nd Street, queuing up in a long snake of a line curling through the terminal, and waiting endlessly for buses backed up one after another in the Lincoln Tunnel as they shuttled us day workers home. All excitement taking place in the Port Authority bus terminal, the launching pad for the points west of New York City. A friend calls it Port Atrocity, though she's being far too generous. The Port Authority is a beast of a building. Its low-hanging particleboard ceilings seem seconds away from collapsing, and the flat fluorescent lighting makes everyone look as though they're in the end stages of liver failure. All in all, a fun end to the day.

Making it back to Matt's house in time to have dinner and hang out with the boys (all four of them) meant that I had to leave work around six thirty. I'd never gotten up from my desk that early in a decade. Not that most of the people were still in the office then. *BusinessWeek* was family oriented, and plenty of folks left around 6 P.M. when they weren't on a deadline. It's just that I wasn't used to being one of them. I scheduled interviews on the West Coast in the evening. I caught up on reading earnings reports. I waited until my girlfriends, all working hard on advancing themselves, left their own Midtown offices at 8 P.M. I had no clue what I would do if I didn't work late, and I had never made an attempt to figure that out.

This devotion to career was reinforced every day by one of my bosses. Amanda was on her way to the top of the ladder (although she would tumble back down amid rumors about Machiavellian strategies gone awry). Trim and in her early forties, she ostensibly lived in California but in fact spent 75 percent of her time in New York. She arrived at the office at 7:30 A.M. and left around 8 or 9 P.M. every night. Her workweek seemed to be made up of six days, none of this wimpy five-day nonsense for her. She didn't socialize outside of work, and she rarely strayed from her California/New York circuit. She seemed uninterested in the world outside of the media mecca of Manhattan and the innovation capital of Silicon Valley. Yet, she was far from lonely. She had her husband at home. She had her department of employees, devoted acolytes all, as her social network. She had her office politics and career plotting.

To me, this was normal. After all, she'd hired me after sizing up my own ambitious obsession with work and her ability to exploit it. Amanda would sit me and my other tech colleagues down for cozy chats in her office. She was an accomplished listener though each of her employees quickly learned that much of what you told her was collected as scraps of information to be used to further her career. Still, in exchange she meted out bits and pieces of her strategies for outmaneuvering other depart- ments, cultivating her managers, and furthering our success as a group and as individuals. We minions did advance. It was just that we were always in her shadow and appendages to her ambi- tion. She held everyone in my department in thrall through a combination of charm and intelligence and the thrill of being close to power on the way up. But the real secret, I always felt, was that she made it her business to figure out what made each of us tick and used that knowledge ruthlessly.

For example, I hate to let people down. It's an impulse formed by all my moves as a child, by my drive to be included. One day in August, a couple of years before the cat craziness began, I'd stopped by Amanda's office on the way out the door to North Carolina for a family beach vacation. We had been working on a big project for the magazine, a summer double issue about tech. My entire department had worked weekends and late nights for two months in a frenzy of writing, editing, and laying out pages. I was exhausted.

"Knock, knock," I said. "Just making a last pass to let you know I finished everything and am taking off now."

Amanda wheeled around in her black Herman Miller chair and stared at me. Her eyes were wide with betrayal.

"You're leaving me?" she said in a low voice. She seemed overwhelmed by the project my group was working on. The fact that Amanda the Immutable was exposing this concern scared me silly. *Overwhelmed* and *Amanda* were two words that you never put together in one sentence. She stared at me for a moment and then slowly swiveled her chair back around to her computer with a faint good-bye.

Struck with guilt, I jogged back to my editor's office and told him what had happened. I offered to cancel my vacation and pitch in on other projects.

"I don't mind," I said. I didn't. What was vacation compared to Amanda needing me?

"We can handle it," he replied, appalled by me and our boss. Peter was as work obsessed as the rest of us, but he was still Midwestern enough in his values to believe you should take the time off guaranteed by your contract and healthy enough psychologically to know a line had been crossed. "It's okay. Get going."

I tried. I really did. But I only made it as far as the first Amtrak station stop in Newark before jumping off the train and turning around. Three hours after leaving the office I was back at my desk. Resolute, ready to pitch in. But not for long. It even seemed that Amanda was embarrassed enough by this bit of manipulation to make me leave again the next day.

All of which explains why, the first time I stood up at six thirty and turned off my computer to go home and take care of the kittens, my legs and brain creaked slowly and uncomfortably. I had tied myself to work for so long that stepping outside of it early on the weekdays made me feel like someone who had broken both legs in a huge ski accident and was out of the casts. I was trying to use muscles that didn't work any longer.

As I walked by her office door, open as always to monitor comings and goings, Amanda looked up from some pages she was editing.

"Oh, does someone have a date?" she remarked in a sly tone, waving her pencil coyly at me.

"Nope, just have a few things to take care of at home."

"Oh," she answered with a bright smile and a noncommittal shake of her shoulder-length blond curls. Amanda probably had no clue what those words could mean, and a few weeks earlier, I wouldn't have, either.

The out-of-body feeling continued right up until I reached Matt's front door. Without wasting any time, I walked up the stairs, straight to the kittens who were the cause of all these unbidden changes. Two Spot and Number Three were waiting at the edge of the chicken wire for me. They were always smaller and cuter than I remembered. Number Three put his right paw up on the blue sheet covering their enclosure. Two Spot, directly behind him as though glued to his hip, stared up at me, his huge ears twitching back and forth, torn between wanting to dart off and needing to stick by his braver brother's side. Zero gazed at me from safety just inside the closet, his saucer eyes unblinking.

I stepped away to get their dinner plate ready, opening the cans of food with a whoosh of air as the vacuum-packed seal slid open. Sure enough, when I turned back, Number Three and Two Spot darted back into the closet, just a blur of black and white, overcome with shyness after the bravado of their greeting. I stepped into their kitty haven and lowered myself down till I was sitting a foot away from them, the plate in between us. Our routine. Watching all three approach on their tiny paws and then settle into eating, I felt more responsible for these kittens than for any being I'd ever had in my life. I'd do anything to make sure that they got the right shot at life. Even if that meant facing my own demons.

My shift to leaving work early meant I could spend a good two hours in the room with the litter at night. The kittens started making remarkable progress, led by Number Three. Number Three was so propelled by his curiosity of everything around him—Matt and me, our clothes, hands and legs, the exciting food we'd bring in—that he went from a wild baby to lap kitty within two weeks. He just couldn't help himself. He wanted to sniff your jeans, tap your hand when it was lying on the ground to see if it was a toy he could play with, tackle your shoe as you stood up. He was also, of course, the first one to purr. One evening, I was lying on my side on the ground, stretched out across the enclosure. He'd started liking to walk across me, balancing his body like a tightrope walker as he made his way up from my feet and along the length of my legs. When he reached my hip, he jumped down, triumphant in having made it the whole way without falling. I reached my hand up to give the back of his ear a little scratch, which he let me do. As I kept rubbing, he turned his head, leaning into my hand, and suddenly I felt this distinctive rumbling. I almost stopped, so surprised that he was letting himself enjoy this. He pushed a bit more against my hand, closing his eyes and purring even louder. Two Spot jumped down from his plant and trotted over, convinced that if purring was happening, food had to be somehow involved. He came to a halt when he saw Number Three just standing there next to me. Number Three opened his eyes, spied his brother, and leapt on him, taking him down in one bound.

Two Spot remained as nervous as ever. He shivered, he jumped, he hid. Yet, little by little, he also began to want to be near Matt and me. Unlike his brother, he couldn't do that head-on. He had to work his way up to it. Two Spot would trot by as we sat in the cage, rubbing up against our legs and arms as if by mistake. After eating, he'd sit down nearby to clean himself, ignoring us. Every time he swiped his tongue across his legs or swept his paw across his mouth, he'd inch just a little bit toward us until he'd maneuvered himself to lying against the side of our legs. His cleaning done, he'd lay his head down and go to sleep. There we'd be, stuck sitting in the same position so we wouldn't scare him until he roused himself about a half an hour later from his post-dinner siesta. Yawning, arching his back in a long stretch, he'd pull himself up and walk away to play, never glancing our way, but aware of us the whole time.

Zero, on the other hand, continued to stubbornly want nothing to do with us. Maybe it was his illness, or perhaps it was his attachment to his mother. He'd scoot to the side whenever we tried to pet him while he was eating, walk a wide circle around us when he ventured out into the enclosure to play with his brothers. He was becoming tamer, in his own way; he was finally coming out. But Zero's continued aversion to us humans only made Matt and me more determined to bring him around. We resorted to dishing up baby food to him all the time, tricking him little by little into coming closer. One day, he was so engrossed in eating Gerber mush off the spoon, he didn't notice that I'd led him forward to stand right next to me. As soon as he realized he was close to my leg, he jumped back as if he'd gotten an electric shock and hid in the closet for the next hour. A tough customer in a small package.

The earlier scare over Zero's illness was our first introduction to the most heartbreaking part of rescuing—caring for sick babies. You laugh about these stories after you've brought a kitten back from the precipice. But there's always an edge to your chuckle. Everyone in the rescue world ends up with litters, and rarely are they healthy. Taking them on is so hard that the last thing you ever want to hear from a friend is: "Oh, you know I saw three of the cutest kittens outside today." Because inevitably, the next thing that person will add in a bemused tone is: "It's funny, though. One of them seems to have some gook in its eyes."

Of course it does. And the other one probably has worms and the third has diarrhea. All you can think after your friend casually utters those words is: I've got to get those kittens. Right now. If I don't, they'll die.

Babies outside are ticking time bombs. They get worms, parasites, and viruses from their mothers, the stagnant puddle of water they lap from, or the bird that mom brought back for dinner. Sometimes their immune systems kick in and fight back. But without immunizations, medicine, and clean food and water, too often these kittens develop infections in the eyes, the lungs, the intestines. And they die. Around a third of every litter born outside doesn't make it past the age of one. Every rescuer we met later knew what it was like to have a little one pass away in their house, in their care, in their hands. They had lived through keeping them warm, hydrated, and eating, getting them the right medicines, doing everything they could to avoid the horror of watching a little rib cage feebly rise up and then never move again. There was even a name for the whole ugly scene: fading kitten syndrome.

This was the defining moment for Alisha, a woman I met later who was the founder of an adoption group called Jersey Cats. Alisha was raised Orthodox in a Jewish enclave in New Jersey that didn't have a tradition of keeping cats, but she set her own path, going about life with a hip white blaze in her black hair and a Zen-like demeanor. Alisha was all about helping others. Having just moved to Jersey City after breaking up with her boyfriend, Alisha decided to volunteer at Liberty Humane Society, the same local animal shelter that our cat trap–lending friend, Joan, had helped start.

Within five minutes of setting foot inside the shelter on her first day, Alisha was led by one of the workers up a dark, narrow set of stairs to the isolation room where the sick cats were held. The worker brought Alisha over to a crate. A litter of four kittens huddled together.

"These ones are really sick. They can't stay here. There's too many germs," the woman explained. "Can you take them home to your house?" She stared at Alisha. Saying no didn't seem like an option.

Alisha, who had never had her own pet, who thought she'd volunteered to spend some time petting purring cats, returned home that afternoon with a carrier full of sick kittens and a metal holding crate. After installing the litter in the cage, Alisha felt bad about keeping them enclosed, so she opened the door to let them wander in and out. The effort was doomed from the start. Coming home from work each night, Alisha would find little trails of diarrhea all over her apartment. Tracking them down, she'd discover the kittens hidden in the corners, under the sofa. When a sick cat starts hiding, usually they are looking for a place to die. Alisha didn't know that yet. She'd move them back into the crate onto the soft bedding, near the food and litter. Each time they'd drag their little bodies out in search of a dark corner. On the third night, Alisha picked up one of the babies to put it back in the cage. The kitten's body was squishy, and the animal began yowling as soon as she was touched, loud and anguished, as if the act of being held was excruciating. The little animal turned her head, bit Alisha, and then collapsed, dead.

Alisha lost it. Hysterical, she put the body down on the ground, rushed to the bathroom to wash her hands, soaping them up again and again and running them under scalding hot water. It was eleven at night, but she called Scott, a former boyfriend who lived in Greenpoint in Brooklyn, sobbing over the phone. Scott immediately said he'd come over. The subway ride took an hour. During the wait, Alisha sat on the couch staring at the corpse lying small and still on the floor. The first thing Scott did when he arrived was pick up the body and put it in a shoebox out of sight. He stayed with her that night, sleeping on the floor.

Alisha didn't give up on the litter. She had taken them on, she would see them through. She just couldn't bear to have any more die in her apartment. When a kitten became immobile and close to dying, she'd rush it over to the shelter, often late at night. Alisha did this twice until she was left with one baby—a little being that ended up making it. Alisha kept this stubborn being, who she named Omar, as her own, a totem to life.

Tragic stories like Alisha's are why many people trap. To keep kittens from dying.

Though Matt and I hadn't heard any of these stories yet, we knew by instinct how lucky we'd been to catch Zero's illness before it got worse. Now that he was a healthy, round little white mouse of a kitten, he still didn't care much for us. But we loved him for the survivor he was.

Yet, as the kittens advanced, I felt as if I was falling backward.

I was alone for hours, shut up in a room in New Jersey,

staring at the walls. Matt was on a tight deadline at work, which meant he was stuck at the office until 3 or 4 A.M., ferried home by taxi through the Lincoln Tunnel after the bus stopped running. Those long nights and the enjoyment he took in working in the early hours made me feel more on my own than ever. Matt loved solitary work when he was deep in a project. The habit was a holdover from his days in school. He and his fellow students were creatures of the architecture world's culture of all-nighters, leaning over their drafting tables until they dozed off, slipping from their tall metal stools to the ground with a thump. This quirk was charming when it was just a story told over a beer. But it was annoying to live with up close.

Especially since I was in the middle of attempting this work/life balance everyone was always talking about. The thing was, there didn't seem to be much of the "life" part happening in this balance. Somehow I'd jumped straight to the slog of responsibility. A week of tending to the kittens on my own, seeing Matt only during the rush to work in the morning, bled into another week. Then, even those conversations during the commute to Manhattan ended. Matt flew off to the Midwest where he was designing the office campus of Abercrombie & Fitch. I was alone.

Matt called the second evening to check in. He laughed about the lithe, energetic twentysomething employees roaming the office campus. Matt's job was to inspire them to creativity and community through exposed wood, light flooding through massive metal windows, and crackling fires in an outdoor fireplace his firm had built next to the company's bus stop. I'd seen photos of the work his group had done. It was an idyllic work compound, surrounded by trees and fields.

I hung up. It was 9 P.M., and I was still in the kittens' room. I walked over to the window. Through the wall of trees across the street from Matt's house, I could see the Empire State Building, a blur of white lights fading and reappearing as the leaves shifted in the wind. That was my city, drifting on the night horizon, out of my reach.

I walked back and looked down at the kittens. They had collapsed, asleep on the soft heap of towels in the closet after filling their tummies with food and running around like demons. Number Three was on the bottom of the pile, with Two Spot curled up in a ball, his head buried in his paws, Zero lying stretched out next to him. Zero had adopted the quieter Two Spot as a surrogate for his mother, trying when he was falling asleep to nurse on his brother's tummy. Two Spot would fend him off by kicking with his back feet, but his only real defense was to curl up tight. The adorableness of this moment was almost physically painful.

I headed downstairs, wandering into the kitchen, aimless, tired of watching TV by myself night after night. I walked to the back door, which we could look out of now that the sheet had been taken down. Oona was a circle of white near the back wall, sleeping among the dark green shadows of the plants. I had worried that she would desert us after we snatched her kittens. For two days, she paced around Matt's backyard and the neighbors' yards, searching, searching, searching for her charges with plaintive mewls, until she eventually gave up. Was she heartbroken? Practical? Accepting? I couldn't know.

163

I read the experts—animal behaviorists wagging their fingers at us poor humans—who warned against projecting human thoughts and emotions about a situation onto an animal, about the mistake of anthropomorphizing them. Cats, one expert explained, forget other cats—even their own litters—after a few days, after the scent of the other animal begins to disappear. I was torn between wanting this to be true, relieved that it could be so easy to shrug off such a physical family connection for lonely Oona, and wanting it to be false, because I was saddened that nature should opt for such a cutting form of amnesia. All I knew was that I felt less guilty the day Oona stopped her wandering and came back to eat by the back door for the first time in forty-eight hours. Maybe she understood our intentions better than I and had decided to stick with us. Or maybe she was hungry.

So there I was, in a half-unpacked house, with a half-present boyfriend and half-tamed kittens. How was this ever going to work? The career and the city-dweller life that I had constructed for myself with such deliberate steps over the past few years was going on without me a mile away in Manhattan. I was stuck in a middle space that I had propelled myself into with an impetuousness I now regretted because I had no idea where it would end. I hated uncertainty. Yet, I had chosen it.

I turned to head back into the living room and spotted a bottle of wine on the kitchen counter, shoved up against a row of cookbooks. It was open. I'd had a glass this weekend with Matt before he took off for Ohio. I looked at the wine, considering it.

For the past few years, I'd been able to take or leave alcohol, just another part of a good dinner. But now, feeling lost in New Jersey, I stared at the bottle and felt its pull, the dull comfort it could provide.

I had a bit of a history with alcohol.

I should ask an airplane pilot sometime: Do you get into a nosedive and then stall or do you stall and then drop into the dive? In the summer of 2000, not just one, but two of the reliable, smart, and thoughtful fellows that I had been interested in only to brush off as soon as we started dating were on their way to getting married. Not to me, just to clarify. I'd tossed away many, many boyfriends on two continents, but this time I wasn't bouncing back.

Life had been trying to tell me something. I had responded with fantasy. After learning about the impending nuptials, I stopped going out with friends. Instead, on Friday nights after work, I took the B or D express train home to the studio I was renting at the time in Greenwich Village. I would come up out of the subway, stopping first at Barnes & Noble at the corner of 8th Street and 6th Avenue, then heading to the back of the store where I picked out four or five romance novels. This could take some time, because not just any escapist, titillating, bodice-ripping story would do. Being a writer, I wanted these stories about the Regency duke wooing an independent bluestocking, the rampaging

Norman knight who turns compassionate about the Saxon village and earl's daughter he ravaged, to be well written. That takes some looking and a subtle contortion of standards.

Books chosen, I stacked them on top of one another, turning the cover with the women in their diaphanous gowns and heaving breasts facedown. Walking with purpose, I tackled the biggest hurdle of this operation: the cashiers, the sole witnesses to my shame. The first few times, they simply rang up the books without a comment. But after a while, we started to recognize one another. I began matching their name tags with the books on a nearby shelf that featured the staff's highbrow picks of new fiction writers, biographers, and quirky graphic novelists. And I could tell they began to realize that I bought the same kind of book in the same quantity weekend after weekend. We had to subtly agree to not acknowledge what was going on while greeting one another with a loaded friendliness.

After saying good night in a studied, casual voice, I would slip out the door and cross the street to McDonald's, where I ordered a Double Cheeseburger and a large order of fries to go. A stop at the local wine store to buy two bottles of red completed my list of errands. And then I went home, where I wouldn't emerge for the next forty-eight hours, wine drunk and awash in predictable stories where the arc of challenge and conquest always ended in "happily ever after." Then Monday would roll around, and I could lose myself again in work dramas.

At the end of a six-month haze of greasy food, literary escapism, and sleep-deprived hangovers, I found myself, yet again, standing in front of the wooden shelves of romance books on a

Friday evening. Outside, the world was emerging into spring. After weeks of the dead gray skies and black uniforms of winter, light breezes, optimistic flowers, and women in flirty dresses were out in full force. I stared at a row of Julia Quinn books. I'd read every single one of the twenty novels lined up on the shelf. Same for Lisa Kleypas's spicy collection. I scanned all the books. I'd bought nearly the entire section, my more sophisticated fiction standards having fallen away months ago. I was so bored with my boredom. So sick of my numbness and my pathetic weekend routine. I picked up a book and then put it down. That night, I went to the movies, escapist still. But this time I went to bed sober at eleven.

That's when I found my therapist, Susan, and even started going to my appointments with her. After canceling enough times at the last minute, I began to realize that if I had to pay the $150 fee anyway, I might as well just sit in Susan's office. Not that this led anywhere at first. I lied for the first six months before Susan made me start telling truths. She pushed me to think of myself outside of my routine.

"What do you want out of life?" she prodded.

"But I have what I want."

"Maybe you don't."

"Why on earth would you say that?"

"Well, what about your bouts of sadness?"

"I just get depressed."

"Exactly."

"Exactly, what?"

Soon I began to see her point. At first, she convinced me to act like a "normal" single person, even if I didn't feel like one. I began to get out of the apartment, go to brunches, see plays, visit museums, and discover the person I could be on my own. I started considering who *I* wanted to be, not what other people expected of me. It had been a struggle, this attempt to create new patterns of behavior, this process of defining myself for the first time in my life, to be at ease with the parts of my existing self that I liked. I'd written down that list of what I wanted out of life, that damn "bag of goodies" Susan had pushed me to articulate. Setting down those words, those wishes, "boyfriend," "roots," "a life outside of the office," "a horse" (really), had been an exhilarating, frightening exercise. Staring at it after I'd written it, I'd cried.

"What if I don't get these things? That will be even worse, now that I've told the world that I want them," I'd said, looking up at Susan in anger.

"There's no reason you can't have them on your own terms. But maybe you won't want them after trying them out. The point is to try. Not getting them isn't failure. It's just experience. It's just life."

Now, here in New Jersey, five years after starting my journey with Susan, I was taking some of the biggest steps yet. I was sloughing off some of my most engrained habits—never leaving work, the last bit of distance I'd maintained between myself and Matt, responsibility for another being (three, in fact).

I felt lost, unsure that I was capable of accomplishing this biggest jump yet. Especially since I was stuck in this house without Matt and alone. Again.

I grabbed the wine bottle and a glass and went in to watch TV and get drunk. All that week, night after night, I fell into a routine, and I kept drinking. My schedule was custom-made for this oblivion. I came home from work, put in my kitten-training hours, and headed downstairs to the one thing that was keeping me company: red wine. For dinner, because there wasn't a McDonald's hamburger to be had in Union City, I opted for microwave nachos.

All I needed to trigger this pattern was being in the room with the kittens. I loved them, but I begrudged them the responsibility they made me feel. I hated that they needed me, that I couldn't give up on them. I hated that Matt wasn't there with me. I didn't have the right to resent them, staring down into Two Spot's huge baby eyes, trying to lure Zero out of his box with yet another spoonful of Gerber baby food, avoiding Number Three's swatting paws. Yet I did. I approached the cage each night and stared down at them, assessing the trio from a distance like a clinician. As if I wasn't the person who had rescued them out of concern and compassion, but just a caretaker stuck in a house I hadn't chosen, walled in by stacks of boxes that made me feel claustrophobic.

One evening, Number Three sashayed forward, all eager for some playtime, with Two Spot following behind, his ears twitching wildly as he struggled to balance his love for me with his natural shyness. Even Zero deigned to walk over to the side of the enclosure, hooked on the promise of Gerber baby food. In just three weeks, they'd transformed. They weren't babies anymore. Their legs were stretching out, their bodies were longer and leaner. They were still adorable, but they were just on the verge of passing out of the round, tumbly stage and into becoming young, small versions of the handsome cats they would someday be. I stepped over the fence, sending them scattering. But they circled back around as soon as I placed their dinner plate on the floor and sat down cross-legged. After polishing off a mound of wet food, Number Three clambered right into my lap, marching around with his sharp claws until he'd tortured me enough and found a good spot, curling up next on my right knee. With Number Three settled in and out of jumping range, Two Spot walked forward on soft paws, tucking his body into the space under my left thigh. Zero, who followed Two Spot everywhere, stood looking at the three of us for a few minutes before heaving a sigh and giving in with disgust. Without looking at me, his eyes locked on the top of Two Spot's ears, he inched forward step-by-step before collapsing on top of Two Spot. Number Three's purring, loud, ostentatious, and carefree, quieted octave by octave as all three brothers fell into a deep sleep. I was surrounded; my resentment waved a white flag of surrender. I loved them so much.

Which, of course, made me feel guiltier still about how trapped they and this house made me feel, and more in need of a drink.

I was a responsible drinker. I would *only* down three glasses of wine each night. Around eleven, after watching some TV, I stumbled upstairs, took two aspirins, and set the alarm. Each morning, I woke in time to feed the kittens, get dressed, and guzzle a bottle of Gatorade with more aspirin and a banana, the electrolyte-potassium hangover antidote I'd perfected. Then, still a bit fuzzy, I would head for the bus stop and work.

I hated this pattern I was developing, but I couldn't stop myself. One evening, I poured half a bottle down the kitchen drain at the beginning of the evening, committed to getting myself out of this rut. For two hours, I watched *House*, made an actual meal of pasta Alfredo, and paced, humming Charles Trenet's "La Mer" to myself. I wanted a drink. Or rather, I wanted to feel numb. It was a beautiful July evening, so I sat for a while on the front steps, watching the violet sky of summer fade after sunset. The street, for once, was quiet, all the mad rushing of cars up and down the hill stilled for the day. Joggers sped by on the sidewalk, focused on the rhythmic swing of their legs. People out with their dogs meandered along the Palisades underneath tree limbs heavy with summer leaves. The cracked bricks of the stoop were warm beneath my legs. I watched tiny red clover mites hurry along the stone, busily searching out food, mates, a place to sleep. Being outside during a perfect July twilight and seeing people happy in the moment should have inspired me or lifted my gloom. Even just a bit. There were other ways of living, of being if not at ease than not as lost as I felt. It would take just a little shift in my outlook, one that I had been able to make before when I'd fallen lower than this.

Union City, in its own way, was trying to give me a push. There was bedraggled charm to this place, to its enveloping insulation. I had been wrong about the town, mistaking its cracked sidewalks, scraggly trees, and dusty buildings for uncaring neglect and isolation. People cared, they just didn't have the means to change much. But knowing I was wrong and that there was a community out there that knew and watched over one another didn't help me. Because I couldn't help myself. I couldn't pull myself out of this sense that when I felt lost, when I didn't control the direction my life was going in, I didn't have what it took to see myself through uncertainty. All of my life, I'd worked to avoid situations where I couldn't direct the outcome. Messy things, like relationships and the feelings of another person. Or responsibility for another being who might act unexpectedly or differently than I liked. When I was uncertain, I buried myself into something I knew and could master. For the past few years, work had been the hole I'd thrown myself into. That wasn't an option now. I'd committed myself to the kittens.

I wanted a drink. I went back inside, got a $20 bill out of my wallet, and, locking the door, set out to find an open liquor store.

Let's go out for dinner. Let's have Mexican." Matt was back from Ohio. "Guacamole, enchiladas, margaritas!" Matt had gone to grad school in Texas. A real evening out to him meant tortillas and salsa, the spicier the better.

"Sure," I agreed a bit fuzzily. What a coincidence: I'd just downed a couple of shots of tequila on the sly in the kitchen before Matt got home from the airport. I was excited that he was returning but nervous that the routine I had established for dealing with the house and Union City while he was away was about to be upset. I had forgotten what it was like to have someone home at regular hours. And there was no way I was confessing to him that I was drinking alone.

We jumped in the car to go to Charrito's, a Mexican place in the nearby town of Weehawken. With its Day of the Dead masks and flags, it was the kind of touristy restaurant you find in strip malls. Despite its Hispanic community and Matt's high hopes when he'd first moved here, Union City had no good Mexican restaurants. People in our neighborhood ate dinner at home. If we wanted to walk to a good Mexican meal, we needed to get friendly with some family. Or drive to Weehawken where a Mexican couple from Union City had started a restaurant for people outside of Union City.

During dinner, I got Matt caught up on the kittens' progress, filling him in on their exploits.

"Two Spot is on the verge of purring. He doesn't know it yet, but he's starting to put out his neck when you scratch him there, so it's just a matter of time," I explained.

"I can't believe how far they've come," Matt said. "Purring kittens, cats on your lap, Zero out of his box . . . It's great!"

He looked sweetly into my eyes and smiled a quiet Matt smile that usually made me feel like everything was right with the world because everything was right right now with us. But instead, I felt sick. Sick from my margarita, from my anxiety, from my dishonesty. At the first sign of trouble, I'd begun sliding down a familiar slippery slope. All without warning Matt what

I was going through emotionally, or how I'd chosen to deal with my sense of isolation. I thought I was making a decision for myself, but looking across the table at him, mariachi music blaring, I realized that any choices I'd made were choices for both of us now, for our relationship. And I had no idea how to tell him.

10

Cherchez La Femme

Detective novels and cat rescue share a central theme—that of the mystery woman. She is a shadowy female who doesn't want to draw attention to herself but is working in the background, impacting the events around her. Our street had its own mystery woman: the feeder. The invisible people feeding colonies of cats on the street are almost always women, alone. Compassionate by definition and crafty by necessity. She is someone who learns to feed her charges at odd hours of the night or morning or away from the prying eyes of neighbors and passersby because you never know how people will react. Often the feeder is a bit (or more than a bit) paranoid, feeling the weight of the cats' survival is on her shoulders. The last thing most feeders will do is tell others what they're up to for fear someone will try to make them stop or do something to harm the strays and feral cats so many see as pests to be eradicated.

This was the mind-set I was up against in my search.

After two weeks of intense work, Matt's project was winding down. He was back home and on nightly kitten duty once again. When I'd been the only one socializing the boys, I had pushed my thoughts about the mysterious feeder to the back of my mind, but now that I had more time on my hands at night, I couldn't shake the notion that finding the person who was feeding the cats in Matt's neighborhood would help me unravel a lot of questions I was struggling with. If I could find this caretaker, I could learn more about Oona's extended family and get an understanding of just how many ferals there were wandering around Manhattan Avenue and whether they really needed my help. Perhaps trapping wasn't always the answer and I wouldn't need to commit myself to this larger cat-rescue crusade I had begun to learn about. Perhaps once I met this mystery woman, I could figure out what to do with my three kittens and, with a clear conscience, take back my life in New York City.

I could also maybe sweep away this nagging drinking habit I'd cultivated by focusing my energies on this search. Drinking on the sly was inconvenient. I had to open the cabinet door in the kitchen above the stove and take a few swigs when Matt was busy upstairs. More than once, I barely got the bottle back in place before he'd troop in. As careful as I thought I was, I still tripped up. One evening he pulled out the tequila bottle, which he hadn't touched in weeks.

"Whoa, whose been making margaritas without me?" he joked.

Caught off guard, I stared at the bottle for a minute before admitting, "I had a couple while you were gone."

"A strong couple, it looks like," he laughed, pouring himself a drink. "Can I make you one now? Maybe with a little less zing?"

"No, I'm fine," I answered in a rush, too fast because Matt gave me a glance across the counter as he squeezed some lime into his glass.

It did look suspicious. We rarely drank much at home, but when we did, we both would have a glass, standing right here in the kitchen at the end of the day. It used to be fun, a shared moment of sending our brains a little off kilter together. Now all I could think about was how to cover up what I was doing on my own. I studied the bottle. Maybe I should start adding water so the drop in level wouldn't be so obvious? As soon as the thought popped into my head, I caught myself. Taking a few sneaky sips was bad enough, but doctoring bottles? I was inching along the edge, peering into the abyss, swinging a foot over the side to see what it felt like, not committed to the jump. Something was holding me back from really doing any real damage to my life or to myself. I was tethered to solid ground, a thin, fine filament attached to me that had never been there before. When I leaned forward a bit, just to test it, it led right back to Matt.

It was Tony who gave the feeder's secret away, ironically. A week after Matt's return home, we were walking home on Saturday from Hoboken when I saw Tony standing on the sidewalk across the street from his house, gazing up at a tree. He'd become suspicious of us since I mentioned that Matt had been to a cat-trapping workshop, but he couldn't help being his advice-giving, talkative self.

"Well," he said, without preamble. "I hope you've given up that cockamamie idea of fixing the cats around here."

This block. What was it about this block? Spend any time here and suddenly you're inducted, without a vote, mind you, into an extended, nosy family. It's not just that everyone knows one another's business and discusses it. It's that they feel they should have an opinion about your actions and tell you what they think. For your own good. In the South, your neighbors gossip about you but never say boo to your face. On the West Coast, they wonder about you but wouldn't dare to judge. In New York City, your neighbor doesn't even know you've lived next door for the past decade. This was so *New Jersey* and its mix of German certainty, Italian bossiness, and smothering Latino sense of family.

"How are you, Tony?" I said, tartly.

"I'm fine. Came over to see if the peaches had ripened yet," he replied, gesturing toward the tree branches above us.

We waited. With Tony, there was always a story.

"It's not my tree," he laughed, pleased he'd stumped us. "The folks who live here know I get peaches off it. I've been doing it for years. So, what about the cats?" In this family, it was okay to chitchat after the opening salvo, with the understanding that you'd get back to the matter at hand.

It was also true that sometimes it's better for family relations not to spill everything. I diverted his attention. I filled Tony in on how we had caught the kittens and brought them inside. Catching on, Matt explained about the magical taming power of chicken dinner baby food and how they were *almost* like tame cats now.

"We're really, really busy with this project," I added.

"Well, good, I'm glad you've given up on bothering the other cats," Tony said, making the leap I'd hope he'd take. Tony wanted to believe that we'd taken his advice. He looked at us sternly. "These cats want to be outside, catching mice, having babies." Point made, worries mollified, Tony gave us both a sudden smile.

"Who wants to taste some wine?"

Tony led us across the street and down a narrow, breezy alleyway to the back of his house along the Palisades, stopping to unlock a green wooden door on the bottom floor. As he walked into the dark interior, Matt and I both glanced at each other. Was this just some elaborate scheme for trapping us so we could never trap cats again? More polite than I, Matt took the first step forward. At that moment, Tony flipped on a light switch to the right of him. Christmas string lights wound throughout the basement storeroom twinkled on, revealing the biggest collection of junk I'd ever seen. Even more than at Matt's place. Milk crates, bottles, planters, tires, old dressers, and chairs were stacked throughout the room. Dusty picture frames, vases, books, bowls, and baskets lay on top of every available surface. A cramped corridor wended through the junk, splitting off into different directions based on no obvious logic. Tony led us down one offshoot, back to the left corner where a squat winepress sat on a wooden table. The press itself was a small, round barrel, clamped together with three metal bindings, with a handle above it that you turned to squash the fruit and a little spout where it came out. The table was lined with bottles of wine.

He turned to present one to us.

"I make all my wine here, with my own grapes."

This was about more than just hauling junk back to a lair. This took a lot of work. Tony was creative. This jumble made sense to him; it was his art. At least, I hoped that the thought that had to go into making this wine also meant there was some sense behind all of this beyond just run-of-the-mill hoarding. He proudly opened a bottle, filled three plastic cups, and handed them around. Union City had more secrets than I imagined. I toasted him, drank a sip, and tried not to spit it out. Pure vinegar.

"Incredible," I managed. What I had here was old-fashioned plonk. A for effort, but the follow-through was no Chianti. We were still solidly on Manhattan Avenue. In a way that was a relief. And charming. I was coming to realize I didn't want this street to stretch too much beyond its shabby boundaries or take on airs. We talked for a few more minutes before saying we needed to get home. As we left, he pressed another bottle into Matt's hands, explaining it was from last year and that he'd love to hear what Matt thought of it once he had tried it. Better him than me, I thought, as I walked out the basement door.

That's when I saw it.

The alleyway that we had walked down to get to Tony's basement also led to his next-door neighbor's yard. I was looking directly at that neighbor's back patio. Sitting on the ground was an oversized metal bowl, mostly empty, though some pieces of orange and yellow cat food were scattered around. There wasn't a feline in sight. I knew right away what I had discovered. This big of a bowl, it could only be something used by a cat lover. I'd found our feeder, the person who was feeding the cats on the street.

I managed to keep it together as Matt and I walked home, waving to Tony, who watched us from the sidewalk in front of his house, whispering to Matt what I'd seen. No sooner had he closed the door at home than I started jumping up and down.

"We found the feeder, we found the feeder!"

"Well, you found the house of the feeder," Matt corrected me, laughing. Which was true, but not for long. I walked to the garage two doors up the street and, flagging down Carlo, the mechanic, had the name I needed in no time.

Hanna.

The next day, I walked down the street and opened the heavy black metal gate and walked up the eight concrete steps that led to Hanna's towering wooden door. I knocked hesitantly. No answer. I rang the two bells on the left of the jamb, not knowing which apartment was hers. There was some shuffling behind the door, and a hand appeared on the other side of the glass, pulling back the white lace to reveal the face of an old woman. She released the fabric, turned the lock, and there she was. Hanna. A tiny figure, straight backed, in her eighties, her hands creased and onionskin thin.

"Hanna?" I asked.

"Yes, dear," she answered in a voice tinged with a German accent. It was a sure voice, a warm one. Though she was small, that sound and the way she stood there in a comfortable silence that followed made me want to like her right away. I was still worried that I had to be very careful about how I approached Hanna. After all, things with Tony, who had the same background and had lived here just as long, went badly after I mentioned trapping. Maybe Hanna would feel the same way. If she did, I'd have to figure out what that meant.

"My name's Heather," I said, putting out my hand. Without hesitating, she grasped it in a papery cool, certain handshake. "I live down the block. My boyfriend bought the house with the blue door a couple of years ago."

"I know that house well," she said, smiling, acting on what I would learn was her natural hospitality and trust in people. "Come in, dear, since you're new to the neighborhood."

Hanna stood aside, waving me into her parlor off the hallway, shuffling behind and directing me to sit down in a French blue wingback chair. An identical chair sat across from it, a wooden table with a lace runner and tubby white porcelain lamp carved with painted birds and flowers parked between them underneath the big front bay window.

"I'll get you something to drink," she said, shushing my protests as she walked through the dining room that opened onto the living room and then to an old-fashioned kitchen at the back of the house. I looked around. Hanna had sturdy, heavy furniture, the kind that had sat in the exact same spots for decades. The place, with its high ceilings, was huge and immaculate, not a smidge of dust on the collection of porcelain statues of animals and children that dotted the side tables around the room or on the beige pile carpet. Yet Hanna lived here all alone, her husband dead, her son occupied with his young family in Central Jersey, according to Carlo, who knew everything about everyone on the street.

Sitting across from each other, the wood table between us topped with a lace doily and rows of framed pictures of her grandchildren, I told her about me and Matt, where we worked, how long we'd been together. She watched me with her alert blue eyes, never interrupting.

The whole time we talked, as she explained how she'd moved to this house from Hoboken with her husband fifty years ago, laughed about how her German relatives spent most of their time when they came to visit in her little kitchen, staring at the New York skyline ("They're there when I turn out the lights at night and when I walk into the kitchen in the morning"), and described her grandsons ("Michael takes after me. I spent the night at their house recently and the next day, Michael was waiting for me at the bottom of the stairs with his little rollie luggage packed, declaring it was time he and I went home so we could get some more good German chocolate"), all I could think about was how to bring up the cats.

I made a couple of weak attempts.

"Do you have any animals, Hanna?"

"No pets in the house now, dear. I'm too old."

A little later, I informed her that Matt had cats. That we loved them.

"Oh, cats are wonderful."

This was going nowhere. Hanna was definitely a cat woman.

She knew not to bring up the topic in uncertain company. Too much talk led to too many people calling you crazy.

We had been talking for about forty-five minutes, and I still didn't know what to do. Hanna asked me how I liked the street. I could have given a pat answer. With her, though, I felt like saying what I honestly thought.

"Sometimes I like it better than others," I admitted.

"I understand," she replied. "It can be lonely." She paused, studying the photos of her grandchildren for a moment. "You have to take the good with the bad, dear. Now, have another chocolate," she ordered. If anyone knew loneliness, it was an eighty-five-year-old woman living her last years in solitude in a house on a cliff.

Now or never.

"Hanna," I said, "we just took in three kittens from outside. They were so wild when we caught them, but they're becoming friendly. They're the sweetest things. I understand that you feed cats outside?"

The clumsiest segue way ever. Hanna sat watching me, her gaze open, unchanging.

"That's right," she affirmed. "Ever since my husband and I moved up here."

"Well," I took a deep breath, deciding to just spit it out. "Hanna, would you be interested in us fixing those cats?" I started talking more quickly, wanting to explain it all at once so she couldn't say no until the end. "We've been learning about how to take care of cats, how to get them fixed so they don't have any more kittens. We don't take them away," I hurried to reassure her. "We bring them right back from the vet and put them out where we find them." I paused. This was it.

"Would that be something that you might be interested in, if we did it for you?" I stopped talking, having nothing else to say.

Hanna paused, studying me. Was she offended? Did she think I was being pushy, judgmental, just plain wrong?

"What a godsend," she said, her faded blue eyes starting to water up. "I watched those little kittens get sick and die for too many years."

I had my answer. Now Matt and I had some real decisions to make about just how far we'd go with trapping cats, how big a commitment we felt like making to this street, this woman, this place.

The other female I had to come to grips with was Oona, the kittens' mother. According to the rescuing material, cats are kitten-producing machines. Matt and I didn't understand just what this meant until a week after capturing the boys. We were jolted awake in the middle of the night by eerie keening in our backyard. Cat voices were echoing across the courtyard.

Opening up the window and looking out back, we spotted two felines we had never seen before in the shadows below. They were hunched face-to-face on the wall, edging each other back and forth. A flash of white emerged from the little cat house downstairs where Oona lived. The cats, growling in low voices, jumped down and sprinted after poor Oona as she leapt up on the bench by the back door and to the south wall, disappearing down the alleyway. Over the next few nights, it was bedlam out back. Strange cats showed up from all over Union City, chasing Oona.

These were tomcats. Oona was in heat.

If I had had any doubts about whether we should keep trapping, these nighttime battles ended it. If we didn't do anything, Oona would soon be in the same situation she was when we first saw her, with another litter of kittens and dangers facing her. We have a lot to learn from animals, and the lesson that was getting through to me most was: spay early, spay often.

On the same weekend that I found Hanna, Matt and I trapped Oona. It wasn't that hard. This femme fatale lived in Matt's backyard, and she liked to eat. The morning of the trapping, we didn't feed Oona. She stalked the back door, meowing at us each time we walked into the kitchen. She was used to a prompt breakfast, and our restaurant was getting sloppy.

I waved at her through the glass. "I'll get some nice tuna for you later," I promised. She berated me in response with annoyed meows.

When we opened the door later that evening to bait the trap we'd left outside to get her used to it, Oona was waiting. She jumped up onto the round metal top of the covered hibachi and then up onto the back fence, watching as Matt put a plate with tuna at the back of the trap and then set the release. Dribbling a bit of oil along the front of the trap and tossing out a few chunks of fish in front of the opening, he stood back to survey his work.

"T minus ten and counting," Matt said.

I looked up at Oona, still hunched on the concrete wall, eyeing the trap.

"Oh, I hope it works," I whispered, worried that it would. I had never trapped a cat with the intent of holding it in a basement, taking it to the vet, and ending its ability to have babies. The rescue folks said cats would thank you for the operation if they could, but I wasn't so sure. I don't know that you'd go around thanking folks for cutting up your stomach and removing organs. Yes, it meant the cat didn't get worn-out by pregnancy year after year, but the drive to procreate was basic. Maybe they meant that *after a while* the cats wouldn't be mad at you. Or if they could understand the big picture they would thank you.

We retreated inside, and Oona jumped down into the yard. Hungry and used to being pampered twice a day with food, she was willing to put up with some nonsense to fill her tummy. She circled the trap, nosing the metal mesh, nudging the plate through the bars with her paw. She circled the trap once, twice, a slow inspection. On the third patrol, she sniffed the tuna juice and gobbled up a bit of fish lying on the ground.

"Come on, Oona," Matt whispered next to me.

One hesitant paw at a time, she walked into the trap, stopping in the middle to eat another bite of tuna. We'd never fed her fish, holding off for just this moment. It must have been a revelation, because she took more steps, inched toward the plate at the back, and lowered her head to gobble up one, two quick bites. Finally, the taste was too much for her, and she settled in to eat, crouching her body down. With that last small movement, she stepped on the trip plate and set off pandemonium. The trap closed with a thunk, Oona spun around, trying to leap out the front, but instead whacking her head straight into the now-closed door. She wheeled again, throwing her body against the back of the trap. Matt slid open the kitchen's back door and ran out, sheet in one hand, as she continued thrashing in the cage. The next moment, he laid the fabric on top of the cage. As he pulled the sheet down over the back, I got a last glimpse of Oona, her light green eyes wide and wild, her white nose bloodied.

With one last heave, the horrible noise of Oona throwing herself around inside the cage stopped.

"That was about the worst thing I've ever seen," I said from the top of the stairs.

Matt let out a deep breath, shaking his head. "I don't know how people do this all the time."

We'd found a low-cost spay program that offered subsidized coupons that you took to a nearby vet for a $65 operation. After keeping Oona in the trap overnight in Matt's basement, I loaded her up into the car at eight in the morning and shuttled her to the vet in Hoboken. The receptionist asked me in a concerned voice whether I wanted to do blood work, which they recommended, to make sure she wouldn't have an adverse reaction to the anesthesia. Did I want additional pain pills to give her after the procedure? Should they vaccinate her, give her a rabies shot, give us an e-collar, test her for feline leukemia and AIDS? Check her teeth, her fecal? Out of guilt for what I was doing to her, I said yes to every question. The bill came to $400.

When the vet called me at work around ten to tell me they also wanted to give her a pill to immediately kill the fleas in addition to the long-term flea ointment medicine I'd already okayed, I called Joan, my mentor in the world of trapping.

"Should I do it? Does this cost four hundred dollars every time?" I asked. "How do you afford it?"

"How much? That's crazy! Where did you go?" Joan replied. When I told her the name of the vet, she couldn't stop laughing.

"Congratulations. You picked the vet with the best racket in the area. I never go there."

As I hung up the phone, it sunk in. We'd been had, taken in by an office who understood how to guilt novice rescuers into running up their bills. This was another lesson. TNR could also be a very good business.

Back home after the surgery, we had to keep Oona in the trap for three days to give her time to heal. I hated this part, too. Surprise. Oona was always so immaculate and jaunty, her coat white like an arctic fox. Huddled in her trap downstairs in the dark, covered by a sheet to keep her calm, she was unhappy and pathetic. I decided to compensate by making sure she was well drugged, pouring a liberal amount of medicine into the wet cat food I gave her every morning and night.

There's nothing quite like having a feral animal crouched in anticipation in a trap in your basement, just waiting for its chance to bolt. You can't just pick up your cat from the vet and stow it away until it heals a bit. You have to feed it and change the newspaper in its cage when it goes to the bathroom, which is a lot grosser and full of danger than scooping litter, because you have to open up that steel trap you caught it in. Not that you give it an open hole to run through, of course. You place a big metal fork through the middle of the cage to create a temporary barrier so you can open the trap. Seeing a potential opportunity to escape or just show you what it thinks of what you've done to them, a lot of ferals swat at the fork with heavy paws and sharp claws or charge at it, with you stooped down behind it, your face inches away from an angry cat.

Oona didn't do any of this. She was cannier. Each time I peeked in on her, she would mewl at me in a sad, low tone. I nearly took her out back to release her the first night after we picked her up. I stomped upstairs, the sound of her plaintive cry echoing in my head.

"We should let her out, Matt," I announced at the top of the stairs.

Matt was becoming used to me blurting things out without any preamble. Not even looking away from the Yankees' game he was watching, he responded, "No."

I shook my head in disgust as I watched him pick up a tortilla chip and dip it into some salsa, and then I turned to clump back down to the basement and stew in anxiety for a while. Of course, it was a stupid idea to let her out hours after her operation. At this moment, she was still loopy from anesthesia. She needed two or three days to recover from the surgery and for us to monitor her to make sure nothing had gone wrong. I sat on the stairs, staring at Oona's trap.

I would have felt responsible for any cat I'd just tricked into having this operation. But during the past month, the tentative connection I'd felt with Oona had become knotted tightly. My bond to her was another thread that kept me from tumbling over the edge. From a wild unknown who'd rushed us to protect her kittens, she'd become an animal that recognized me. That's what that little meow meant. One of the amazing things I'd learned was that cats don't talk to one another, just to people. Hiss, yes, meow, not so much. Maybe I could try to socialize her? It's something I'd considered. But even if Oona never swatted me, she still bared her teeth and backed up when I got too close. I had never touched her. Her fur might look like down, but I had never brushed my fingers across it to know what it felt like. She knew me, but she was still wild.

Sitting there on the basement steps, looking at the green sheet covering her cage, trying to imagine what she was going through, I understood that she had a better chance of survival now that she wouldn't give birth to kittens every few months. But was that good enough? She was going back outside, to the traffic, the street, the noise, the fear.

Rescuing is this weird world where you try to balance being happy that you're doing the best you can with an intimate understanding of the hardships that strays face. That's why you make the effort. You begin to pay attention to what these animals are going through, and you are impelled to act because you realize that feral cats are a human creation. They're domesticated cats that escape or are put out, and that, over time, slip the harness of human attachment. Yet, their ties aren't severed. They continue to coexist around us, to depend on us for food, whether through someone who feeds them or by scavenging our trash. After a generation, they grow to fear us, but they need us just the same. It's rare for a colony to exist on its own through hunting. We are their keepers, whether we pay attention to them or not.

What you're doing when you trap these animals is triage in a crisis. Some strays will lose their fierce ways and come back into the human fold, but most are too unused to humans to become domesticated, and there are just too many of them. On Matt's street alone, I'd spotted fifteen cats. You deal intimately with animals that look like the cuddly felines we know and love. Yet, you have to treat them as the wild beings they are. You can't get attached. You create a distance. You respect them, are compassionate, and let them live their own lives. I'd have to let Oona go for this to work.

It turns out it's tricky to drink while you're shuttling between a cat that's looking for ways to escape out of its trap in a basement and a trio of circus kittens in your second-floor office. I know. I tried.

On the second night of Oona's return from the vet, I arrived home in a foul mood made worse by a last-minute call from Matt saying he was staying late at work. Again. His defensive tone, his apology for calling late and for not knowing what time he would make it back, made the whole conversation worse. It was nearly 8 P.M., and I'd just spent an hour and a half getting home. The line for the 123 bus at the Port Atrocity had been the worst yet. The buses for Union City kept not showing up. What made it more galling was watching people headed home to Hoboken, the town down the hill from Union City, troop onto a constant stream of buses that all left half empty. Richer, with million-dollar brownstones and investment bankers, Hoboken had much better transportation than Matt's scrappy little city on the Palisades. The buses shuttling the nurses, bus drivers, and restaurant workers back and forth from Union City to New York were always crowded. Tonight was no exception. It was standing room only by the time I handed over my ticket. Jammed between a teenager blasting hip-hop through his earbuds and a construction worker who piled his bag of tools right next to my legs, I lurched through standstill rush-hour traffic, knocking my shins against a power drill.

I burst through the door, heading straight for the kitchen, and had a drink. Gathering the kittens' food, I steeled myself and went upstairs. Radio, Matt's cat, had developed a bad case of jealousy. Now that the kittens were friendlier, we'd recently started letting them out of the chicken wire enclosure so they could wander around. Radio had spotted them one day through the doorway as we'd gone in, and he'd become obsessed with them. He'd taken to sitting on the wooden floor outside the kittens' room and sprinting in to scare them whenever we opened the door. Two Spot, nervous to begin with, took this terrorizing the worst.

Tonight, I was surprised and relieved to see that the landing was vacant. One break at least. Radio must have given up for the night. I placed the three cans of food and spoon on the floor in front of the door and opened the door. That's when Radio struck, rushing through the doorway of the next-door bedroom and into the office. Number Three, who had come to the door to greet me, fled back, leaving Zero behind and unprotected. Radio ran straight for Zero. A big, long tabby, Radio hovered over the little kitten flattened to the floor, whapping Zero's little head with a massive paw. I ran forward, enraged and shouting, and as fast as he'd appeared, the big cat turned and darted out of the room.

I slammed the door shut. Zero popped up and skittered to the closet. In the complete stillness of the room, I slapped my palm against the door. Stupid cat, stupid Matt. If my supposed boyfriend had been home, like any normal human being would be after eight at night, he might have been able to stop his green-eyed monster of a pet from rushing in and scaring the hell out of the kittens. As it was, I wished I were the one who wasn't here. All I wanted right now was to head straight out the front door for the bus to Manhattan and never return. I was stuck.

Feeling bitter, I walked over to the closet to check on the kittens. Zero had buried his body into Number Three, who was also taking refuge in the cardboard box. Zero wouldn't let me touch him, but his eyes were open and seemed unscratched, and he wasn't bleeding. That was the good news. The bad? Two Spot was MIA.

"Two Spot, here little guy," I called, opening a can of cat food. Number Three and Zero, with the attention span of the babies they were, put the incident behind them as soon as I put a plate of food on the ground for them. Waving the empty can around the room didn't tempt Two Spot out of whatever hiding place he'd found. I looked behind the boxes lining the walls, underneath the futon, and in the closet for fifteen minutes before sitting down on the couch, worried and racking my brain for where else to look.

"Mewl." A torn weak cry coming from behind where I was sitting.

I twisted around.

"Two Spot?"

"Mewl." There it was again, louder this time.

I got up and walked toward the wall and the line of metal cabinets. He couldn't be between them. After the time that they'd hidden themselves in a crack, Matt and I had pushed all the cabinets together. Two Spot's meows were definitely coming from the cabinets. Was he inside them somehow? If I opened the wrong drawer to find out, would I hurt him? As I studied the cabinets, Number Three, done with dinner and on the prowl, jumped from a chair next to the windows up onto the sill running the length of them, prowling over to where I was standing. Then I realized what might have happened. The sill was close enough to the cabinets that the kittens could jump onto them.

I grabbed the chair and put it next to the cabinet. Craning

my head over the top, I looked down behind the cabinets . . . and there was Two Spot, stuck in the space between the back of the shelves and the wall, staring up at me with his huge eyes. He was hanging in that space, unable to get enough grip to pull himself out of the hole.

"Poor guy," I murmured, reaching over to cup him underneath his tummy and pull him up. As soon as his paws were high enough, he scrabbled onto the top of the metal. Without hesitating and just as I suspected, he dashed across the row of cabinets, leapt onto the windowsill, barreled into Number Three, and jumped down, disappearing into the closet under the safety of the curtain.

I went downstairs for another drink.

Some pasta and a little more wine later, I remembered that I'd forgotten to feed Oona. Hoisting myself off the couch, I stumbled against the sofa table. Three drinks in an hour and a half had made me more than tipsy. I hadn't been this unstable in a long time. I considered waiting for Matt to get home, but it was almost 10 P.M., and I hadn't heard a peep from him. That silence was telling. He'd probably be at the office later than late. Which created a problem. Oona couldn't wait until morning. She had to have her pain medicine. I set out for the basement on clumsy feet. I stepped down each wooden step as if I was ninety years old, my hand hooked around the smooth wood banister. At the bottom of the stairs, I sat down to give my head a minute to settle and tried to put her medicine in her food. On the first try, I squirted the liquid over the top of the bowl, launching an arc of sticky brown liquid onto the floor. On the second try, I managed to aim the syringe of medicine at the wet glob of chicken meat in the bowl. Folding back the sheet covering the front of Oona's cage, I contemplated the trap, sure that I was forgetting something. Ah. The metal fork. I swung around, spied it leaning against a crate, and picked it up with a loose wave of my hand. With a wobbly push, I inserted it through the top of the trap. I was set. I unlatched the rear door and pushed the bowl inside.

"Hello?"

Matt was home earlier than I'd thought. I slid the door flap back into place, pulled out the fork, and pulled the sheet back over the end of the cage. Somehow I'd finished my chores. I made my way one step at a time back up the stairs. Triumphant.

"Hello to you," I said, hoping the words sounded normal.

"Big day on the project. We finished the punch list!" Matt laughed.

I didn't respond.

"Listen, I am sorry." He walked over to me, picking up my right hand and pulling me toward him. "I know you're sick of doing all this on your own, but I got everything done tonight so I could take tomorrow off and spend some time taking pictures of the kittens." His brushed his hand up my arm, a caress soothing my rigid tension. "I know you worried about finding them homes. This way, we can start bombarding everyone we know with emails of adorable kittens."

This was the thing about Matt. Just when I felt the most misunderstood by him and justified in laying distance between us, he reached across that barrier to show me how much he wanted to make me happy. I *had* started becoming concerned about the next step for the kittens, though I hadn't had time to think about what to do about it. I'd been too caught up in trapping Oona, in finding Hanna, and in worrying about when my sudden need for alcohol-induced fuzziness would end.

With his hand resting warm and solid on my arm, I felt how tired I was of worrying about being lonely. And tired of using alcohol as an anchor to sink me deeper into that loneliness, allowing myself to ponder in the basic reality we all know: that we are alone. Of course we stand singly in the world, but accepting this, knowing that it can offer strengths. My time with the kittens, Oona, and Matt was showing me that being aware of ourselves as individuals can help us better see the beings around us and what connects us all. I could see it, I had seen it. My old fear about my ability to be at ease with shades of gray, rather than the black or white dichotomy I had always resorted to, had tripped me up. I had been content many times with the kittens before allowing myself to fall back on worrying whether I could keep being truly happy with them. Matt and I had made this cat project happen though we'd been novices in working together on something that had consequences outside ourselves. We'd figured out how to pull together, but too often I'd concentrated on the points where we'd struggled back and forth instead of our moments of triumph and collaboration.

I needed Matt. Not because he was someone who could save me—I didn't need saving—but because he was the person who saw me, my compulsions, and my insecurities and accepted them as part of the entire person I was. Who knew that the cynical girl he loved, who made him laugh with her rants, was made up of compassion and energy and fears. He knew it better than I did. He helped me see it.

Exactly like today. He'd known that when I started making kvetching noises about finding homes for the kittens, soon it would blow up into full-scale worrying, but that he could harness that energy by helping me. By taking photos of the kittens and taking steps toward solving the problem at hand.

I stood staring at Matt and his funny big forehead, his crazy short haircut. At the beginning of every summer, he gives himself a buzz cut, as if he were a sheep that needed shearing for the warmer months. The first time he appeared with his summer look, walking down 75th Street to meet me outside of my apartment on the Upper West Side and go out to dinner, I took one look at him and walked back into my building. I didn't recognize him. He'd become some Southern boy straight out of the 1950s. All that was missing was a short-sleeve white button-down shirt and a letter jacket. When I finally realized who I was looking at, I'd hated his complete transformation from the wild-haired fellow I'd met. Now I love it because it's one of Matt's rituals, like the way he sits down and does nothing for ten minutes before starting off on a big trip or how he makes lists for absolutely everything.

I knew I could confide in Matt about the drinking. I knew he wouldn't judge. I also knew I didn't need to tell him if I felt there was some unresolved issue that we needed to deal with. There wasn't. The kittens coming out to greet me, my ability to handle Oona, Matt's pleasure in helping me—everything that happened tonight were things I could choose to be connected to in the moment, or I could make the decision to see things in a negative light, to set myself apart in my frustration and create that distance I was so comfortable with. Either path was my choice, and it was time to accept the good with the bad, to adapt and move on, and to begin looking for the links that helped me define myself and yet feel connected together and alive in the moment.

I'd struggled with my demons and dulled them with a few too many drinks. I knew I would again someday. But I understood how to quiet them.

Matt would help me, too. I did need help, though not with the same worry that a few days ago had seemed to consume me about my resentment of the cats and whether or not I could even handle the responsibility of caring for them. Those thoughts, I realized, had turned out to be just a sideshow. I needed help with practical, everyday things like kitten taming and deciding what to do about Hanna, the feeder. Things that no drink could help me accomplish. And all I had to do was ask for it.

"Matt, I've been drinking a little too much tonight, and I just don't think I can change the paper in Oona's cage. Do you think you can take care of that?"

He laughed, just as I knew he would, and went downstairs without a word to do my bidding.

"Wow!" I heard him exclaim.

"What, what?" I said, rushing to the top of the stairs and peering down.

"Are you lucky," he said from the bottom of the stairs. "You forgot to latch the cage. Oona could have snuck out, no problem."

I smiled. He looked up at me, baffled.

"Is everything okay?" he asked.

"Yeah. Yeah, I think it is now," I said, realizing that yes, I was okay, that this self-destructive routine was over because I didn't need it anymore.

What a pair we were.

Four days after catching Oona, early in the morning, Matt hauled her and her trap up the wooden basement stairs and out back. After a couple of days of brutal heat, we had a break in the weather. It was warm at eight in the morning, but not so stultifying you didn't want to move. Matt placed the trap down on the concrete, aiming the front toward the south wall and the gateway into Roberto's backyard so she could run off without having to jump the fence and put pressure on her dissolvable stitches.

He folded the edge of the sheet back and waited, giving her a chance to get her bearings. From underneath the shelter of the green fabric, Oona craned her head around, darting looks at the sky, the fence ahead of her, us standing next to her. Matt bent down, unhooked the latch to the door, slowly pulled up the metal door, and stepped back. Oona leapt forward and disappeared into Roberto's lot. These traps were like starting gates at the Kentucky Derby.

Matt looked over at me and smiled. All Oona knew was life outside. This was where she belonged, despite what I might hope. Now at least she would have a few less things to worry about. I knew I would be smarter next time I had a cat fixed. I also knew I couldn't have done anything different this time. And I was going to take care of Oona from now on. If she would let me.

I stepped forward and threw my arms around Matt, happy. I hadn't known what I would feel when we let her go, but I found myself overwhelmed by relief and a sense of how right the world was at this moment. I hugged Matt tighter, grateful for smell and warmth of this man I'd spent so much time avoiding and, at the same time, hoping to find.

After discovering Hanna, I wasn't about to let her go. I spent many afternoons with her. She always greeted me with "Hello, sunshine!" and a welcoming tug of the elbow, urging me to come in, come in, sit down, and have some chocolates. There was always a pile in the frosted glass dish on her sofa table.

"That's what they are there for," she scolded me when I tried to hold back. "You have to enjoy these things now. If you don't, when are you going to?"

Hanna was alone. Her husband, Johan, had recently died, though it wasn't his passing that left her by herself. He was too mean to miss, she would say. It was more that Hanna had been on her own all her life. She knew heartache. In the border shifts after World War II, when lands were being split between Poland and East Germany, her German family was expelled. Then, at twenty-one, she bribed a guard and darted across the border to the west, urged on by her mother to leave her and a sister behind and make a better life with an aunt who lived in the United States. Hoboken, New Jersey, to be precise. She learned to read and write English in six months but ended up marrying a German nevertheless, a choice she came to regret.

Hanna moved with her husband to this house on the Palisades in the 1950s, overlooking a cascade of trees, the flowing Hudson River, and a stunning view of the Manhattan skyline that was too often just a sad backdrop. She had lived there for fifty years, raising a son, hoping for another child but then giving up that desire as she realized that her husband didn't love the one they had.

"My husband's father bought this house for us," Hanna said one afternoon, when I asked why she moved here. "It's a million-dollar view, but they can have it. I never wanted this house and then, there you are, after all these years, it's mine."

It was a stifling August day, the air on the street parched, struck still by the heat. But inside Hanna's darkened house, the lace sheers drawn, the windows in the back and front opened and ushering in a cross breeze, it was cool and calm. I had stopped by at the end of the day on a Saturday after playing with the kittens.

"Johan's father was gone on the boats out of Hoboken when Johan was growing up," Hanna explained. "And his mother ran around. She didn't care about him. That's why he was the way he was with his son. He never got any love from his own family."

I looked around at the high ceilings of this peaceful room, an old TV sitting in the corner across from us, the heavy wood hutch next to me stuffed with porcelain Hummel statues from Germany, little hand-painted figurines of pudgy young boys and demure girls who had witnessed such a common tragedy. Hanna never left because that's not what you did then. And she was afraid she would lose her son if she did. She stuck it out. The first night she got out of the hospital after she had a mastectomy to keep her breast cancer from spreading, her husband demanded dinner. He'd said that one day he was going to put the house in her name, too, when his father turned over the deed to them, but then came downstairs later, drunk, and said he'd reconsidered.

"I've been waiting all my life. I sit here waiting," Hanna said as the early-evening light settled around us.

That was what was so remarkable about Hanna. She faced the sadness threaded through life, but she was determined to be upbeat. Hanna kept busy, patching her own concrete walls outside; climbing up ladders to clean her windows even though she'd been forbidden to do so by her son; and planning trips to Hanna Krause, a chocolate maker in nearby Paramus that ran a candy store that looked straight out of the Black Forest.

And she stayed loyal. To her son and his young boys. To her family in Germany, who visited her often, staying for weeks. She was always on the phone with her friends, urging a bedridden woman from church not to worry, everything would be fine.

Laughing with Steve, a neighbor she took in as her own son decades ago, during his calls from Portland to check in on her.

"I'm the only real family he has," Hanna had explained to me after one call with Steve. "When his mother up and left, he was standing there staring at the refrigerator, tears coming down his cheek, and I said, don't you worry, Steve, you can always come to our house. He reminds me that I darned his socks after she left, and I say, yeah, because you were too cheap to buy new ones."

For the past thirty or forty years Hanna had made her way down her back stairs every morning at eight to feed the feral cats, finding them sitting patiently outside the back door. The cats had been the constant in Hanna's life. She had watched the families expand and collapse over the years, new cats arrive and stick around, others wandering in and out, or dying. They depended on her, trusted her. They showed up whether they were sick or well, in snow or sun. The cats and Hanna were there for each other. She never thought of not taking care of them.

Looking down from Hanna's back kitchen window a few weeks after I met her, I saw her colony. She said she had about a dozen now. I spotted a slim black-and-white cat that looked just like Oona, two calicos, and an all-black one with just a splash of white on the tip of the tail. One of the mothers had had a litter earlier in the summer, Hanna said. But the three kittens died, their eyes caked with goo.

"When did you start?" I asked, wanting statistics like reporters tend to. But Hanna didn't deal much in facts.

"Oh, that was many years ago," Hanna replied. "I just

always loved animals. That's the way the world is. You know me. I'm such a softie."

Which was true because she was an equal-opportunity feeder, welcoming the groundhogs and the raccoons.

"Tony says they eat the kittens," I said to Hanna, gesturing at her masked customers.

"Oh, him," she scoffed. "I think the animals are smarter than humans. He just says that so he has an excuse so he can trap the raccoons. It's lousy. He gets a kick out of it."

I asked Hanna if I could watch her feed the cats the next day so I could see how many there were. The following morning at seven forty-five, I inched down the alleyway beside her house, coming to stop right before the gate that led to her backyard, hunching myself up against the wall so that the cats wouldn't notice me. There were three lined up outside her back door, the two calicos and the black-and-white ones that Hanna said were the friendliest. During the next ten minutes, five more showed up, picking their way through the overgrown grass in her tiny yard, so intent on food they didn't notice me. And then a gray cat ambled by in the alleyway, rubbing up against my leg before squeezing under the gate. This, I remembered her saying, was the pet of the former superintendent of the little apartment house next door. He put the cat out when he retired to Puerto Rico.

The back door opened.

"Hello, sweethearts," Hanna called out in her strong, even voice. She shuffled forward, holding a plastic pitcher full of food in one hand, a cup of water in another. The cats kept a distance but churned at her feet, wanting to rub up against her but unable to overcome their fear. She leaned over, dumping the food and water into the empty dishes sitting on the concrete patio, and stepped back, gazing down at her brood.

Feeding was Hanna's act of faith, despite a lifetime of disappointments. Watching her, the morning still cool and quiet, I saw that hope could appear in the unlikeliest moments, through the fragile connections we make with those around us and in the will to keep believing in life, even if you have little to justify that faith at times besides a bunch of cats that keep coming back.

11

The Weight of Forever

By the middle of August, the kittens were as ready as they'd ever be to be adopted out. Number Three was the star pupil, with Two Spot a close second. Zero, however, remained a problem child.

Nothing explained the kittens' personalities better than how they played with toys, in particular Da Bird. There are many toys you can choose for a cat, but nothing matches Da Bird. It seems innocuous at first, just your run-of-the-mill toy with a feather hung by a string to the end of a thin metal pole. But there's something in the swing of the cord, the slight bend of the pole that sends that feather swooping and flipping and zipping around that it makes the kittens crazy—in a good way.

At least it did once they got over their total and absolute fear of toys.

A couple of weeks earlier, I had been lying on my side in the room with the three boys gathered around in their usual post-feeding comatose haze. Two Spot was lounging on top of his beloved spider plant, his tail swishing over the side of the pot. Number Three was lying at the base, swatting at Two Spot, while Zero was splayed out next to the wall. I reached up and grabbed Da Bird, which I had left on a table when I brought in the food. I unfurled the string and the feather at the end and began swishing it slowly along the ground toward the boys.

"What do you think . . ." I started asking them.

Two Spot eyed the moving feather with horror, frozen in place. Number Three's eyes widened to enormous round dials. Then, total chaos. Two Spot rolled off the pot right on top of Number Three. Number Three, who had just jumped up, tumbled back down. Zero looked up from where he'd been snoozing, terrified. There was a moment of thrashing legs, and then Number Three and Two Spot managed to stand up, gave the now-still feather one last wild-eyed glance, and dashed into the closet. Finding himself on his own, Zero followed up the rear with a desperate scrabble of paws. Within a minute, the only sign of life was the swaying blue sheet.

Bewildered, I looked down at the pole in my hand. What kitten doesn't like a fishing pole toy?

Previously wild ones, I learned when I went downstairs and reported the whole flailing limbs and widening eyes incident to Matt.

"Oh right. That class I took, Neighborhood Cats, mentioned something about that. Kittens don't know how to play at first."

"They played all the time outside."

"I mean, playing with humans. And these kinds of contraptions."

"I thought kittens liked feathers."

"I bet they do. But they're probably more used to seeing them attached to a bird. Maybe one feather, drifting down on a string, is a little strange for them."

"That's disappointing."

"You should keep trying. Maybe give them something else to start with. I remember Neighborhood Cats saying that when the kittens do start playing with you, it's a big breakthrough. It means they're coming to trust you. You're not just bribing them with food. You're interacting with them."

"A breakthrough? Hmm."

I walked away to the kitchen, determined. I was shuffling through bolts, notepads, and old keys in the junk drawer looking for potential kitten toys, when my hands stilled. Matt had just played me. I liked to win. When I was a little kid, I used to throw board games up in the air when I lost, sending red and black checkers zooming around like saucers. Matt knew me, and he knew what he was doing: I needed that breakthrough. I was set on getting the kittens to play with me.

I decided to start small. I figured that I would stick with the basics, not complicate things too much. Upon reflection, a flashy multicolored red, blue, and yellow feather dangling from a red line was probably too much for toy novices to handle. After all, the only feathers they had seen had been light gray (according to Matt, who had seen Oona carting a couple of doves back to the yard to do a show-and-tell with the kittens in preparation for their hunting days).

The next night, while Two Spot and Number Three sat grooming themselves next to me (and Zero across from me, because on principle he would never choose to sit next to me until later in the evening), I retrieved a bit of beige cotton string from out of my pocket. I placed it on the ground next to where the kittens were sitting. They just looked at it. I tugged one end of it toward me, inching it back. All three jerked their heads back, staring at the string like it was a live snake. I moved the string again, expecting them to dart away. Number Three decided to stand his ground, so Two Spot, after moving his eyes from his brother to the cord, became brave enough not to move. Zero, ever Two Spot's sidekick, had no choice but to stick around as well. He wasn't happy about it, though. I waited a minute and then wiggled the string. Two Spot cocked his head sideways, beginning to consider the slim thread of cotton with some curiosity rather than pure fear for the first time, while Number Three continued to stare it down, determined not to retreat. For three long minutes I wiggled the string around. The kittens never relaxed (and Zero, petrified, didn't so much as move a muscle), but they'd made the decision to stay where they were and watch.

The next night, I couldn't wait to get back to Matt's to try again. After dinner, I sat down cross-legged on the scratched wood floor, the bit of string concealed in my hand. When I put it on the ground and moved it, the scene was a repeat of the night before. Three kittens jumped back slightly, but they didn't leave. I dragged the bit of thread across the ground for five minutes. By now, the trio was following its movements with their heads, swinging them slowly back and forth as I swished it along the floor.

The next evening was a huge breakthrough. We'd settled into our pattern of me wiggling the string, maybe two inches of movement to one side and then two inches to the other at the most. No wild swinging here. More like a puritan string. Then, with a quick jab, Number Three thrust out his right paw. He'd moved so fast, I wasn't sure anything had happened.

Except I no longer had the string.

Nobody moved. Number Three was gobsmacked. His paw was suspended two inches above the ground with the cord swaying off of it. Two Spot, my sweet worrier, had his eyes locked to the bit of thread that was now right next to him. His ears twitched violently in all directions. Zero backed up, looking around. You could see both of them trying to figure out which way they should flee if it started coming toward them.

I waited for Number Three to put his paw down, but he was frozen in place. I was going to have to get it from him. Reaching out wasn't going to work. He'd run, and like any good parent, I didn't want his play experience to end badly. I tried to imagine what a bomb-defusing team might do in this situation.

"Good job, Number Three," I murmured to him. Number Three looked from the bit of thread to me. I kept talking to him in that singsong tone.

"That won't hurt you. You're going to love that string one day. Just not now, I can see that." I reached behind me and grabbed the jar of baby food and a spoon, ever at the ready for situations just like this.

I turned the lid. At the sound of the vacuum seal breaking, the boys forgot about the thread and came racing over, stepping on my legs in their eagerness to get to the baby food. As I fed Two Spot with the spoon, while Number Three stuck his nose into the jar and Zero licked the lid, I reached over and picked up the cord that had fallen forgotten to the ground.

The next night, string, Two Spot, Number Three, Zero, and I were all back in our original positions. String inched itself across the floor toward Number Three, who I was sure would break first. Sure enough, Number Three took a swipe. This time, I held on to my end and started wriggling the thread. Number Three jabbed once, twice, three times, and then, he jumped on top of it. As I pulled it out from under him, it swept by Two Spot, who, seeing that it hadn't killed his brother, whacked it with his paw. Within a couple of minutes, all three kittens were wrestling with one another and me for the string. Wild kittens? You'd never know it.

From the cord, we progressed to Da Bird. Matt got into the habit of playing with the feather toy with the boys each night after dinner. He would sit on the futon mattress slumped over on the floor in the middle of the room and begin swinging the pole in a methodical back-and-forth motion. Number Three was always the first to come over, galloping back and forth, sprinting to make a grab at the feather as it changed directions. If Zero or Two Spot, mesmerized by the gliding object, tried to get in on the action, Number Three would speed up his pace, beating them each time to the feather and jostling them aside, until his roughhousing would force them to drop out, defeated. Alone again in the spotlight, Number Three would relax and become his easygoing self, sprinting back and forth until, exhausted by such wonderful play, he'd walk over and step into Matt's lap where he would curl up and start purring as loud as a car motor.

Only after Number Three had given up the field could Two Spot, who had been waiting with studied patience under a chair, jump in. And he did. If Number Three loved to run, sprint, and gallop, Two Spot adored leaping. Matt would adjust the swing of the feather, sending it flying up higher so that Two Spot could make fantastic air assaults, arching his body in mid-leap to make wild grabs with his long, agile front legs. He was a whirling acrobat who would propel himself off the ground as if he had springs in his legs, snatching the feather out of the air as it whipped in a new direction. Up and down he jumped, until he had also had enough and went to sit next to Matt on the futon.

Zero was a puzzle. The most handsome of the lot, he was also the most reserved. He adored Da Bird, too, but insisted on playing on his own terms. Matt couldn't talk to him or make little encouraging sounds the way he would with the other two. Matt wasn't even supposed to look at him too much. He preferred that Matt just glance at him once in a while, as if the two of them were engaged in parallel playing, like two toddlers building separately with blocks on a rug. He'd grown from an adorable all-white fluff ball into the most beautiful kitten, so small and sleek you wanted to touch him right away. But you couldn't. At the slightest touch of hands around his belly, Zero became all claws and teeth to escape the encircling fingers.

The thing was, he felt an attachment to us. When we were in the room, he'd lie by a wall and watch us the whole time.

215

Every once in a while, just to keep us guessing, he'd show measured affection. He'd fall asleep next to us or brush up against our hands when we were putting food out, as if looking to be petted. But after each brief encounter, he'd run off into a corner to be by himself, as if shocked he'd come that close. With patience, he'd become friendly in his own way, though it would always be on his own terms. Zero was just like that: a complicated soul. There was a connection there that had been won through six weeks of hard work. It would take time—and the right person—for him to come around fully.

The tricky part was we didn't have the time to get him to that point on our own. The kittens were now nearly four months old and growing quickly. Too quickly. The key to finding homes for a stray, we'd been told again and again, was to do it when they were young and cute. Kittens found homes fast. Older cats, not so much. Around the fifth and sixth month, they became lean and lanky, more like adults than babies, and the adorable pull that they'd had would begin waning fast. We were now in a race against the clock. Ready or not, we had to get moving and find them homes.

A t first, the process of adoption was exciting because it was a new role to figure out for us. We were animal saviors now. We hit up our family and friends tentatively at first and then shamelessly, with emails featuring cute photos of the kittens and a paragraph about their background designed to tug at the heartstrings. I tacked up three five-by-seven-inch glossy prints in the lunchroom at *BusinessWeek* and spent an inordinate amount of time hanging out next to the coffee machine and chatting up people. My colleagues only asked if my boyfriend did animal portraits.

We even dipped a toe into the weird, emotional world of pet adoption that is Craigslist. Just for a second. Because after posting a listing for the kittens one afternoon at work, I soon learned that Craigslist was a hyped-up microcosm of the greater adoption world. On one end of the spectrum were the rescue groups with their slightly hysterical posts, warning posters about people who trolled the site looking for free animals to turn over to labs for testing or to use in training pit bulls to fight. We initially neglected to mention that we were charging an adoption fee. I was barraged with emails from rescue folks warning me that I had to amend my post *immediately* to state that the kittens weren't free. On the other end of the spectrum, I fended off younger folks drawn by our litter's cute quotient. As earnest as they were, all I could think when I received a quick email saying, "Luv the kittns!!!!" was that these kids were still babies themselves and in no state to make a decision about whether they were ready to take on a cat for the next decade or two.

The oddest exchanges, though, were with a couple of people who seemed interested, who asked the right questions, and who then stopped emailing all together, not bothering to tell us whether they'd decided to adopt a different cat or had been run over in Times Square by a bus. The intimacy, the hope I had while emailing these folks felt even stranger and more misplaced when they went MIA. Because email is such a fast, off-the-cuff way to communicate, I felt confused, spending hours trying to figure out their motives. Were they window-shopping? Was there something lacking in our kittens? Or were these people just looking for something perfect and therefore unattainable that they thought would make them happy? I couldn't know. The naïve. The rude. The noncommittal. They all found their way to Craigslist. After five days and scores of emails, I felt like I was on Match.com, not the pet section of Craigslist. We decided to delete the post.

The experiment with Craigslist made me come to grips with the full force of what was about to hit us. Accepting that we were going to give the kittens away after spending so much time with them was one thing. Trusting someone else to take them was another. After all, kittens are cute. Nearly anyone will take one home with them. But that's the problem. A precious boy grows up into an adult. One that poops, eats, scratches the furniture, gets sick or anxious, and starts peeing on the bed. Cats end up on the streets or in shelters for one reason: people. Humans don't think through whether they can afford a pet and its bills for the next fifteen years. They adopt the animal for the wrong reason, like wanting to make a darling Christmas gift. Then they inevitably do something like move in with someone who is allergic and decide they have to get rid of the animal—fast.

When we started reading online and asking others how to go about adopting, we got two very basic pieces of advice. Ask for a fee and get people to sign a contract like one you can find online at any rescue group, to weed out people who aren't serious. As we dug deeper, it became apparent that people who rescue animals are often reluctant to believe that humans deserve them. The rules and hurdles of some of the groups we looked into ran the gamut. No adopting to people who have young children, let their cats outside, or are over sixty. No window grate? No cat. Ditto no vet recommendation. Which is a catch-22 if you don't already have an animal. Yet, as paranoid as some of these requirements seem, we understood the concern that motivates them. How would we figure out if anyone was good enough for our kittens? Finding the right place, or a "forever home" as everyone in the rescue community called it, was the most important job of being a rescuer. You didn't want to go through all this heartache and work simply to see the cat end up in the shelter, or, worse, on the street.

It was around this time, one Saturday afternoon at PetSmart on a food run, that we came across something we had never noticed before—a line of metal crates full of kittens. We'd been racking our brains about how to find a home for our boys. This was how one group of people did it. I approached a woman standing by one of the tables. She was tall and solidly built, reminding me of Eleanor Roosevelt with her broad face.

"Um, hello," I said, the only opening I could think of.

The woman turned, taking me in.

"We found some kittens about a month ago," I started explaining, sweeping my hands toward the cage.

The woman nodded, noncommittal.

"We were wondering if you had any advice for finding them homes?"

She smiled a bit, relieved, I later learned when I got to know her. She'd been worried when I approached her that I was trying to give her my kittens. Her house was packed with crates of litters that she'd taken in. If I had asked her, she would have had to wrestle with the question that every overcommitted rescuer faces: Could I fit three more kittens in the bathroom/kitchen/walk-in closet for a while?

The woman apologetically explained that her group didn't have any room for us to show our kittens at PetSmart. She offered to put them on Petfinder, an adoption Web site for non-profits, but we'd already wrangled our way on there through another connection.

"Friends," she said. "If you haven't rescued before, you have a network of friends you can hit up. I've had too many cats for that to work anymore." She laughed. She wrote down her number, asking whether we'd had the mother fixed. She seemed reassured when I said yes. Handing the paper to me, she said to call if we needed advice.

"I can't promise I can help," she said. "But I can listen."

As I walked away, I looked down at the name written out with such precision. Carol McNichol. This slightly harried woman, it turned out, was *the* force of the local cat-rescuing world. A rescuer who was more of a revolutionary, Carol started out as a dog lover. She had helped Joan open the county shelter, cleaning cages, walking dogs. The immediate flood of stray felines that came in—and the fact that 70 percent of animals in shelters are killed—converted her to the cat brigade.

A worker by nature, Carol started trapping. She was incredibly driven, and she escalated to organizing rescuing training, mass trappings, and adoptions. Like any committed animal lover who, by definition, can't set boundaries, she bought a house in Jersey City so she would have a place where she could rescue *more* cats. Carol started the Neighborhood Feral Cat Initiative, a local nonprofit that got grants from PetSmart to run monthly rescue workshops, underwrite low-cost spay/neuter, and help spread the word about trapping. She'd trained hundreds of people and helped fix thousands of felines. Yet, like any leader in a seemingly unwinnable war, Carol never felt that she—or anyone else for that matter—was doing enough. Cat people are odd in exactly the ways people think. They obsessively care for their animals, swapping stories about that hoarder in Union City who had fifty-two cats; the wily, hard-to-trap ferals (always females) who know how to avoid every trap; the stray you catch with the mystery illness that ends up costing thousands of dollars. But they aren't people-hating hermits. They help one another. It's just that cats are the hobby that brings them together, not bowling. Oh, and that they buy a whole lot of kibble.

C arol was right. Our first real lead was some good friends. Matt went through his contacts again and sent an email to Petia and Jose, a couple he'd known since grad school. Matt contacted them on an off chance, but he turned out to be morbidly lucky. Their beloved cat who they'd adopted twelve years ago had just died. This was how Niko, Petia and Jose's precocious seven-year-old son, came to be our first adoption test.

Petia and Jose loved to cook. They loved to get together, to sit down and talk through an evening. Their visit to meet the cats couldn't just take place some day after work and school. They wanted to have dinner, to celebrate meeting the kittens, to enjoy all of us being together. The Saturday after Matt emailed them, they came over toting grocery bags laden with local kielbasa, homemade potato salad, and salad. We supplied the wine.

The first order of business was the initial introduction of the kittens. We adults decided in a quick huddle at the foot of the stairs that Niko should go up with Matt and me by himself. Though the family's other cat had been Petia and Jose's, this one was going to be Niko's. He should have the honor of meeting them first. Niko was a talkative, handsome young boy with short, straight black hair and a friendly, curious gaze. He chattered about soccer, which he adored, as he followed Matt up the steps to the cats' room. Bringing up the rear, all I could imagine was the worst: kittens hiding behind boxes, kittens scratching Niko, kittens just not behaving in general. We'd never introduced any-one new to our trio before, which now, as we were about to open the door, I realized could be a fatal mistake. Things could go very badly.

But they didn't. As we walked through the door, Niko leading the way on bouncing steps, Number Three, who was sitting on the windowsill observing the traffic on Manhattan Avenue, jumped down with a thump and thundered over. He was his usual gregarious self. It wasn't just Matt and me that he liked, it turned out. It was the whole human race. He skidded to a stop in front of Matt, putting his front two paws up on his shins and looking at him with an expectant, mischievous look. Number Three was ready to play, and Matt was his usual cohort. Niko, thrilled, squatted down to pet Number Three, giving him a good scratch behind his ears, admiring his white coat, his wide golden eyes. A regular cat person.

I looked around. Two Spot was also being more outgoing than I'd expected. That is to say, he hadn't jumped behind the metal cabinets yet, and though his big tabby ears were twitching back and forth, he was also walking forward toward us, though on much more cautious paws than his brother. Two Spot didn't come straight across the room. His path took him weaving back and forth, his eager, observant gaze never leaving our faces. I looked around. Zero was nowhere to be seen. It would have been too much to expect for him to be out.

"This is Number Three," Matt said to Niko, making the introductions. "That one over there, making his way to us, is Two Spot, and Zero . . ." Matt paused, scanning the room. He was more surprised than I that Zero hadn't made an appearance, which I thought was generous of him. "Well, Zero is . . . around. They're named after the spots on their backs. See?"

"Oh yeah," laughed Niko. "Mom showed me the pictures you sent. They look just like them. They're so small. And fast!" He giggled as Number Three took a sideways leap to land on Two Spot. Scrambling to his paws, Two Spot ran careening around the room with Number Three chasing him.

Niko loved them. Especially when Matt brought out the feather wand and showed the young boy how they liked to play with it. We stayed with Niko for fifteen minutes, demonstrating to him how loud Number Three could purr when you rubbed him in this particular spot under his chin and how high Two Spot could jump. Zero made an appearance, inching out from underneath the blue sheet in the closet to peer from a distance at all the action.

"He's beautiful," Niko said, spotting Zero right away, as if he'd been waiting for him. He walked toward the kitten, who turned around and disappeared again inside the closet. Turning around, Niko found Number Three at his feet, waiting for him to swing Da Bird again. When we said we were going back downstairs, Niko asked if he could stay with them. Delighted, we left the four young boys together.

Petia, Jose, Matt, and I went out back to set up the tables and start grilling. The backyard, which we'd strung with some Christmas lights, with the table set and candles lit, looked prettier than I'd ever seen it. It was wonderful to sit out at the end of a summer evening, drinking wine and swatting mosquitoes as the three friends talked about grad school and the architectural projects they were all working on. Petia, tall and lean with black hair, was one of those outgoing, inclusive people who had a way of making the environment around her warm, exciting, and full of potential. Jose, just as handsome as his son, was a bit shorter and little less exuberant than his wife, but in a confident, calm way. They talked about working together on local projects, how they navigated working as a team. I gazed at Matt sitting across from me in the fading sunlight. Matt wanted to start his own firm one day. I could see him wondering how his quiet style of dealing with people would work compared to outgoing Petia and confident Jose. I watched him follow their easy back-and-forth and wanted to be able to help him become the kind of architect he wanted to be, as Petia and Jose helped each other.

The whole time Jose and Matt grilled the kielbasa, Niko played upstairs with the cats, dancing out the back door every half hour to give us updates.

"Number Three is up there proudly purring," he announced on his first appearance, proud himself that the kitten liked him.

"Two Spot tackled Number Three and stole the feather from him. He's quick!" he laughed the next time he came skipping outside.

"Zero came out again. He's sitting on the futon watching them. I think this time I'll get him to play with me," Niko declared on his third visit to us adults.

When Niko came down to eat, he sat at the table giving his parents the rundown. I began to notice that many of the questions Petia and Jose were asking were about Zero, which struck me as odd, because he'd been MIA most of the time. Petia turned to me, describing how their previous cat had also been a rescue and how he seemed so much like shy, serious Zero. Their cat had been an underdog, too, just like Zero, Petia explained. Niko watched his mother closely.

Glancing back and forth between their almost identical profiles in the candlelight, I began to worry. When Niko jumped up from the table and ran back inside, I excused myself and said I was heading upstairs to see how things were going.

In the cats' room, I soon realized this adoption event wasn't shaping up the way I'd anticipated. My bet had been that Niko would prefer Number Three, because he was such a rough-and-tumble, friendly kitten. Niko did like Number Three, who was climbing all over him as he sat on the ground, purring whenever Niko caressed him. Yet, after waving the feather around for the bold boy for ten minutes and then holding him in his lap, Niko looked around. Spotting Zero on top of some boxes, he put Number Three down and walked toward the other kitten. That Zero jumped down and skittered away didn't put Niko off. He trailed behind him, trying to coax him out of whichever hiding place Zero found, whether behind boxes or on top of the shelves. Each time that Zero fled, Niko would whirl around to discover Number Three next to him, and he would laugh. He'd play with the gregarious kitten for a little while, but then, as if remembering some important task he had to do, he'd return to trying to woo Zero. Finally, when he found Zero lying in his box in the closet, he crouched down and reached out his right hand to pet the cat. With a quick swat, Zero scratched the back of his hand. Niko looked up, astonished, and then back down at the red mark appearing on his skin.

"Oh, I am so sorry," I said, appalled. "Does it hurt?"

"I'm okay. Kittens do that," he said, as if reassuring himself. Then he proclaimed, "I nearly petted him."

At the end of half an hour, he'd made some headway through sheer persistence. Zero played with Da Bird with Niko for a while, before realizing that he was the center of human attention and flopping down along the wall. Niko sat next to him for a few minutes, watching Zero as Number Three climbed up into the boy's lap.

At the end of the evening, Niko led his parents upstairs to show them the kittens. Petia and Jose laughed about Number Three's outgoing tricks and held him in their arms, petting him, exclaiming about how soft his coat was. They laughed at how Niko could now get Two Spot to jump higher than Matt had ever managed. But it was clear that they were taken by Zero, his deliberate reserve, his beauty, even though the kitten watched us all from the windowsill and wouldn't come closer, no matter how we tried to tempt him with baby food. As they left the room, their last glances directed to Zero, my concern grew even more. On the stoop outside, Petia said Niko wanted to take the night to think about it. He'd told them he was definitely going to take one of them. He was just having a hard time figuring out which one. I couldn't help but worry.

The next day, in a grown-up way, Niko called Matt on his own to deliver his decision. Standing in the kitchen, listening as the two spoke, I couldn't tell a thing from their brief conversation. Hanging up the phone and placing it on the counter, Matt turned to me.

"He wants Zero," he explained with an apologetic smile. We'd talked about my nagging feeling last night, that Niko might want to take Zero because he reminded all of them of their old cat, even though that reserved cat had never been Niko's pet. Matt had held out hope he'd choose Number Three in the end.

"Oh, I knew it," I replied, disappointed. "Zero is all wrong for a child. Zero needs a patient adult and lots of quiet."

I thought for a moment.

"We need to do some adoption counseling," I said, looking at Matt.

Matt was quiet.

"You can't second-guess people, they have their own reasons for doing what they want to do," Matt replied.

"Zero might scratch Niko's eyes out."

"Well, maybe," Matt agreed.

I watched him hopefully.

"Number Three would be a better fit," he said. "It's not right, though, to interfere. Niko's made his choice."

"But we know the kittens better than he does. You saw how Number Three was with him. And how Zero was. He's making this decision based on what he thinks he should do, not what he wants to do."

"You don't know that. You can't. You have to respect his decision."

Matt could seem so easygoing, but he could be just as stubborn as I was.

Zero would probably do fine with Niko, but he didn't have the makings to be the friendly companion Niko wanted. Niko had mentioned last night that he'd already bought a bed for the kitten they were going to adopt, a sort of padded miniature tent. He'd put it next to his bed, giggling about how much fun it would be to have sleepovers with his new friend. Number Three, who adored cuddling, would love that. He probably wouldn't stay in the tent very long, making his way in no time onto Niko's bed, next to his pillow. On the other hand, odds were that Zero, our aloof loner, would end up sleeping under the bed—and never coming out while Niko was around. He'd be a presence, not a body Niko could play with or pet.

As I imagined how the scenario was likely to play out, I became more stymied and frustrated. How could Matt agree that Number Three would be the better cat and yet be unwilling to take the steps to do anything about it? I gazed at him and felt how I could let that frustration grow. Our quest to adopt out the boys was leading us down pathways I hadn't anticipated. We had to make a decision together on something that mattered more than where to go to dinner. In those situations, a credit card bill was all that was at stake. With Number Three, Two Spot, and Zero, we were making a decision about our kittens' lives.

Considering my frustration for a moment, something I'd rarely done before we embarked on rescuing the kittens, I got that here was one of the junctions where I had a choice. I could resort to my old ways and fume. I could try to force Matt into doing what I wanted, which might or might not achieve my aim, but which could create a rift between us, at least a temporary one. Although don't those add up over time? That approach wasn't right anymore, not for me, not for the kittens, and not for my relationship with Matt. Our actions together had consequences. I had to opt for another approach, explaining what worried me and listening to him. Accepting the outcome either way. That last part would be the hardest for me.

I began talking. I explained how I did understand why they liked Zero. How if I'd recently lost a cat, I'd probably also want one just like it. I described how great Number Three had been with Niko, how they'd liked each other right away. I talked about how Zero probably wouldn't be happy without Two Spot, who he was so attached to, and they didn't have room for two cats. I told him how I thought being in a busy household with lots of Niko's friends around might make Zero more nervous, though I agreed that I could be wrong about that, that maybe it would make him come out of his shell. I was worried. This time, it wasn't about me trying to be in control, I managed to laugh.

Then I listened as Matt talked about how thoughtful Petia and Jose were, how they were careful to think things through, and how they wanted Niko to make his own decision. How saying we thought he might want Number Three more might seem like we were telling Niko what to do. We talked for a while in a way I knew we hadn't before, listening to each other from two sides of a fence we had to respect, paying attention to each other's words. In the end, Matt said he would outline some of what we were thinking with Petia, but he wouldn't say that we thought Number Three was better for Niko. I agreed that I'd accept whatever decision Niko made. As Matt picked up the phone to call, I realized that it was true. After talking this through, I would be okay no matter how it turned out.

Petia didn't answer when he called, which made Matt even more nervous as he started in on his message, describing some of our thoughts about Zero and Number Three, which we hadn't discussed with them the night before, though we probably should have, and asking her to discuss them with Niko. We'd be happy with whatever decision Niko made. Either of them would be lucky to be his pet.

Five minutes later, Petia called back and said she understood. She thanked Matt for taking the time to explain more of our perspective about the kittens. Niko had decided he'd like to adopt Number Three instead. He was thrilled, and the sooner he could come live with them, the better. He was sure Number Three would love the tent.

It was as though we'd just gotten a permanent member to change a vote on the UN Security Council. I'd listened to Matt. He'd heard me. He'd figured out a way to approach his friends, to describe our thinking about the kittens' traits in a way that didn't question why Niko's parents had felt such a kinship to Zero. We realized we could do this. We could navigate finding the right homes for the kittens. Together.

I picked up my coffee cup and took a swallow. This was such a small event, a blip relative to all the other big decisions couples made. But it represented so much to me. We could have these kinds of discussions together, though I understood that another time, we might not agree and things might not work out perfectly. I wasn't sure how that would end, whether my mind would explode when it happened. But we had come this far.

12

Total Capitulation

If someone asked you to meet them on 31st Street and 8th Avenue next to Penn Station so they could drive you to New Jersey in a dark red Buick to see some, err, kittens, would you?

Neither would I.

But Katie the Saint did. Katie was a graphic designer living in the farthest reaches of Brooklyn. More crucially, she was a friend of one of the administrative assistants at *BusinessWeek* who'd noticed the photos I'd posted in the pantry. Passing me one day in the hallway, this work colleague mentioned that her friend Katie was thinking of getting a kitten. Could I email her some pictures of the kittens so she could forward them along? Skipping back to my desk, I couldn't hit the send button fast enough. In response, nothing but silence. I figured that, like so many other adoption trails, this one had gone cold. A week later, an email showed up from Katie. Were the kittens still available? They were, but I was beginning to feel that I didn't want them to be, now that the little band had started breaking up.

I had dropped Number Three off at Petia's the Wednesday after their visit. Niko met me at the back door of their white bungalow, pointing out where he had put Number Three's food and water bowl in the kitchen, leading me back to his room to show off the little bed he'd told me about. I set down the purple carrier that held Number Three and bent down to look at the miniature walk-in tent made out of sky blue plush fabric. The pillow-swaddled interior looked like the inside of the bottle in *I Dream of Jeannie*. Up under the dome was a string attached to a dangling mouse. Both Niko and I nodded to each other as we agreed that Number Three would love this tent.

I turned around and opened the door of the carrier. Number Three walked to the edge of the opening, craning his head around to take in Niko's room. He stepped out onto the rug. Niko, on his knees next to the kitten, reached out to scratch him behind his right ear. Number Three leaned so far into the boy's caress that he fell over. Niko laughed. I joined in, feeling bereft. As Number Three made a slow tour of the room, ducking under the bed, squeezing behind some shelves, jumping up onto a table, I looked around. This was now Number Three's home, where he'd come to love Niko and, bit by bit, forget us, his brothers and mother, and his beaten-up outdoor nursery. I had been so focused on figuring out how to get Number Three into the carrier, working out which route to take to Montclair in the car, and remembering to bring the small green towel that he slept on with his brothers so he'd have a familiar smell in this new place, that I hadn't had time to process that this trip, this was forever.

I watched as Number Three walked back to Niko and me sitting together on the rug. He climbed up onto my crisscrossed legs and started purring. For the last time, I picked up my brave, bold kitten, buried my nose into the back of his neck, and passed his warm, small body over to Niko. Number Three settled down into the child's lap.

"I'm going to call him Blacktop," Niko confided, glancing at me to see what I thought. "See how he's got that cool patch of black right across the top of his head? And he's also from the street, right? We've been looking at his pictures a lot on the computer since we got home, and that's how I decided to name him."

"It's perfect," I agreed.

I stood up. Petia, waiting just inside the door of Niko's room, walked with me to the back of the house, inviting me to stay for dinner and spend more time with Blacktop. I declined, saying I couldn't stay. But what I meant was I couldn't bear to.

With Number Three gone, Two Spot became a lovable cuddler of a cat, a kitten that would jump on our laps as soon as we sat down on the beige mattress futon in the boys' room. Zero became a little less aloof, but he was still a stickler for convention, a true New York neurotic. He liked to chase the feather, but only after we sat in the room quietly with him for fifteen minutes. If we placed our hand on the futon mattress just so, Zero would eventually come over and lie next to it and let us pet him. I was sure he'd never find a home. It was going to be just Matt, me, and our strange cat in the front room through the ages. When we died, health officials alerted to the smell coming from the building would find Zero chewing away on our fingers. In his odd, loving way, of course.

The first hint of how interested Katie was in the kittens came when she agreed, without a pause while we were talking on the phone, to cross the Hudson River to meet the boys. There was no way to underestimate what a big deal that was. To New Yorkers, the area surrounding the city was a foreign country that required a passport—one you never applied for because you never left. (Except to visit the Hamptons and upstate New York during the summer, but those places were inhabited by so many other New Yorkers that they seemed like annexes of the city.) I never considered inviting my friends to visit us at Matt's house, because they just wouldn't come. The notion of traversing the Hudson to visit New Jersey was inconceivable.

All of which is to say I was primed to like Katie before I met her. I didn't want to blow the deal by giving her the intricate instructions she would need to find her way through the Port Authority bus terminal or to take the 123 bus to Union City. Instead, I offered to pick her up the following Saturday in the car that Matt's parents had recently given him. Matt couldn't come with me, because he had to work, so this was a solo mission.

We agreed to meet outside of Penn Station. Driving through the Lincoln Tunnel, it struck me that for a car previously owned by a couple in their sixties in suburban Virginia, this long, dark red Buick sedan was *the* perfect New Jersey mob car. As I made my way down 31st Street, I saw Katie standing on the right-hand side of the street. She was a medium-height, slightly heavyset woman who stood with the relaxed air of someone never in a hurry. I pulled to the curb and rolled down the window. Leaning over, I waved to her.

"Hello," I called out, turning the car off so I could get out. I intended to introduce myself on the neutral ground of the sidewalk where she could see that I didn't look like an axe murderer. But before I could turn the handle of my door, Katie opened the passenger door and climbed in.

"Hi!" she greeted me with the genuine enthusiasm I soon learned was part of the Katie package.

"Uh, hello," I responded.

"I am just thrilled to get the opportunity to meet the kittens," she said. "They are the most beautiful creatures. Thank you for coming and picking me up. I can't wait."

With that, we zoomed off to New Jersey, Katie talking the whole ride as if we'd been friends forever. I warmed up to her right away. I just prayed the kittens would do the same.

Back at Matt's house, walking up the stairs, I reiterated some of the points about the kittens that I'd already relayed to Katie during our initial email exchanges. I felt like a broker trying to close a deal. I'd explained their personalities, how both were reserved but that Two Spot became friendly once he knew you. Zero, well, Zero I said was a shy cat. There wasn't any way of getting around it. Katie had said she wasn't sure she wanted two kittens. But since she lived by herself, she did understand that if she had a pair, they could keep each other company while she was gone during the day. I'd made the case for how much Two Spot and Zero loved each other and that taking care of two wasn't much different than one.

Right before we walked into the room, I stopped.

"Katie, Zero's a little . . . particular. Do you think once we sit down, you'd be able to not move for a while? For, say, about fifteen minutes?"

Katie smiled. There wasn't anything behind that smile except acceptance. She seemed okay with odd. When she walked into the cats' room, she was greeted by . . . nothing. They were both hiding. Matt and I had strategized about this meeting, deciding not to feed them much that morning. Opening up a can of food, I placed it on the ground near where Katie was sitting on the folded-up futon mattress.

They emerged from inside the closet, yawning and bumbling forward. Katie oohed.

"They're more handsome than they looked in the photo," she exclaimed in a quiet whisper.

I beamed. I liked her even more for her compliment and for the effort she was making, through her murmurs and stillness, to put the kittens at ease.

Katie admired them as they ate, groomed themselves, and played with the feather pole toy. I wooed Two Spot over to us and showed her how he liked to be scratched on his back near the base of his tail. Even after he kept jumping out of her lap when I tried to place him in it, she was content just to pet him when he was sitting on my knees.

She thought Two Spot was sweet. But I could see that she was entranced with Zero. With his immaculate white fur, deep black eyes, and sweet little triangle face, Zero was as drop-dead gorgeous as Oona. It was love at first sight. As Two Spot made himself comfortable in my lap, Katie picked up Da Bird and started swinging the feather in slow loops in the air for Zero. At first, the kitten ignored the toy. But Katie was so patient and yet so clever in the way that she teased him with the feather, swishing it this way and that, that within five minutes, he was running and jumping in tight little ecstatic circles. When he managed to catch the feather, he'd clamp it in his mouth and carry it away, collapsing on the floor to chomp on it for a while until he'd release his grip and Katie would inch it away from him and begin swinging it around again. They played together for half an hour in almost total quiet until, exhausted, happy, Zero came over and jumped up onto the cushion next to me. Two Spot got up out of my lap, stretched, and lay down to curl up with his brother. The two fell asleep, a warm heap of black-and-white fur. Katie and I sat together in the silence, watching the sleeping boys.

She turned to me.

"I love Zero," she said in a soft, enraptured tone.

I panicked for a moment, worried now that Two Spot would be on his own.

"I would like to adopt them both. How could you ever split them up?"

Exactly, I thought, looking with adoration at Katie.

That was the moment when I realized you can't worry about rescues. All that panic I had felt, the nights I hadn't slept, the feeling I had had that we had made an awful mistake because we would have to split them up, that they would never have a home to themselves, was so much wasted energy. Cats will find a home. The right one, if you're patient. Because there is always that certain person looking for them, searching for them. Some stray kittens will transform into perfect little balls of fluff, playmates for children. But there are always the loners who only ever love one human, the head cases who hide under the bed until after the lights go off and then curl up purring at your feet, the independent ones that never need a human but who are wonders to have around. It's just a question of waiting for the right person who is ready to embrace that animal for who he is.

It was the second Monday in September. We had arranged to drop off Two Spot and Zero (who Katie was going to call Jasper and Theo) at Katie's place in Flatbush at the end of the week. In five days, we would be cat free. Everything could return to how it had been before. We hadn't made any commitments to Hanna about her strays. I could try to get someone else to help her get them fixed, and I could go back to my apartment. Matt's front room could return to being a dumping space for books and office supplies.

We were on our way to work, walking together down the hill

to the ferry in Hoboken. It was an early fall day, breezy and full of possibility. We were floating along because we were kitten-rescuing successes. We'd found homes for our kittens. And not just any homes. Great homes. Marvelous homes. Homes with people who are just as crazy as we were about the kittens. We couldn't believe how lucky we'd been.

Then we heard them. Well, first we saw the cat we'd always just called "That black-and-white cat down the hill." She was a small thing, more hard hips and skinny neck than anything else, but what made her hard to miss was how persistent she was, meowing and walking around our legs whenever we got near her. We saw her all the time on our way to work. We hadn't paid much attention to her, once we saw that she didn't stray far from the front porch of the red tar paper–covered house where she seemed to live and that always seemed to have food and water out for her on the porch.

But this time, as we walked up and she walked meowing toward us, we heard another sound besides hers.

Kitten mewls. Tiny little bursts of noise coming from under the steps of the red house. Confused, we stopped. That black-and-white cat darted from our feet to under the steps and then emerged a few seconds later. She ran back and forth like this for a few minutes. It seemed physically impossible that something this small and emaciated could have kittens. There had to be another mother cat nearby. That black-and-white cat must be a kindly aunt. Matt stepped through the gate of the metal fence in front of the red house and bent down to look under the stairs.

"Huh," he drawled, pushing his head farther under the steps.

"Okay," came a muffled voice. "I don't see the kittens, though I can hear them. Loudly."

He backed out, stood up, and looked up at me. "She's the only adult cat under there."

"Those are Hitler's kittens, all right. You can have them if you want them," said a voice right next to us.

I jerked my head around. Tony, who lived next door to the red house, was standing by his short metal fence.

"Hey, Tony," I replied, pointing to the emaciated cat still circling our feet. "That cat has kittens?"

"Yeah, young ones. The guy who owns the building, he's not too happy about them under the stairs," Tony said. "So if you want them, you can take them."

It was as if we had so many cats in this neighborhood that you could pick them up like a bottle of milk. Except without paying. Or okay, by paying through vet bills.

"I thought she belonged to someone in this house?" asked Matt. He'd moved back onto the sidewalk.

"Nah," Tony explained. "One of the tenants feeds her, and the owner is okay with that. But nobody would notice if you took them."

"They sound kind of young to move," Matt said.

"It's up to you," Tony replied. "Take 'em, don't take 'em. We'll always have more." He turned to walk inside the house. Just as he opened the door, I remembered something,

"Hitler? She's called Hitler?"

"Oh yeah," Tony laughed. "Check out her face. She has a little mustache under her nose. We call her Hitler."

I looked down at her, as she emerged once more from under the stairs. Sure enough, there was a black slash under her nose on the right side of her face.

"Not sure Hitler's the first name I would have picked," I said to Matt as we started back down the hill.

The next day, as we walked by Hitler, I mean, that black-and-white cat, we talked about what we should do. One thing was clear, she was friendly. That meant we could take her in with the kittens right away. If we really wanted to. It would be a good thing to do. But freedom seemed like a good thing, too. After three long months tied down to our kitten routine, we were finally free. We could go out in Manhattan, we didn't have to rush for the bus at the end of the day to play with the kittens. We could even sit in front of the TV and not worry that we should be upstairs socializing the boys. I could patch up my friendships with my girlfriends in Manhattan who I had ignored all summer, go to movies with them or stay out late after work and have a few glasses of wine. Unheard-of things. It dawned on me that we were empty nesters. But decades earlier than most people. We opted to savor the moment and decide this upcoming weekend what to do.

The following day, Wednesday, the choice was taken out of our hands. Summer was back with a jolt. It was eighty-five degrees at eight thirty in the morning, heading to ninety-five. The air was hot and still, the sun glaring down on us as we started our walk down the hill to catch the ferry to New York. When we got to the red house, that black-and-white cat wasn't under the stairs anymore, and neither were her kittens. She'd moved them out into the open, placing two squirming bodies on the bare concrete slab at the bottom of the stairs. Cars were racing down the hill five feet away. The kittens were black, tiny, two weeks or so old, eyes closed, no bigger than mice. They were wriggling around next to the mother who was lying down, looking up at us as we passed. I stopped.

"This isn't normal, right?" I asked Matt. "Mother cats don't bring their kittens out into the open. And it's too hot for them to be out all day. There's something wrong."

Appalled, Matt glanced down at the kittens, his gaze full of worry about what was going to come next. Like he was watching a slow-moving car accident, accepting the inevitability of the crash.

"We have to bring them in," I said, stricken by the sight of the mother and her kittens.

He winced. "I. Knew. It," he managed to say.

Turning on his heel, he walked back up to his house. I raced to catch up.

Matt took the morning off to set up a place for the mother and her kittens in the spare bedroom. I couldn't miss work because Wednesdays were deadline days and I had a story closing, so I trailed down the hill to the ferry on my own, dazed.

My emotions teetered between appreciation for what Matt was doing and disbelief that we were back where we'd started, cat-wise. If I needed proof that Matt was special, here it was.

The tragic part was that my hunch about the litter was right. When Matt picked up the mother, putting the kittens in a cardboard box and her in a carrier, he checked under the stairs and found a third kitten, dead. One of the two remaining kittens, meanwhile, was much smaller than its sibling and didn't seem to eat well. That night, while I was checking it over, looking for signs of an illness, I found worms under its skin. I took the little family to the Cat Practice first thing the following morning. Dr. Sullivan shook his head over the smaller baby. It was infected with maggots through a wound on its back, he explained. He'd never seen anything like it, and there was nothing he could do for the poor thing. We had to ease it on its way. During that visit we also learned that that black-and-white cat was seriously ill.

By now, we called her Eva. She may have started off as Hitler, but there was no way we were sticking with that name. Instead, we decided to name her after Hitler's girlfriend, Eva Braun. At first, we weren't sure whether we should call the remaining kitten, a girl, anything. She was also sick, and it wasn't clear whether she would make it. In a moment of hope, we chose to give her a strong name, to help her pull through. She became Wolfie.

The kittens had suffered because Eva hadn't been able to produce enough milk to nurse them all. Eva didn't have any ordinary illness. Her intestines were twisted to the point where she wasn't getting much nourishment. Dr. Sheheri, the vet who worked with Dr. Sullivan, told us with apologetic fascination that she'd only ever seen Eva's condition in horses. After a long operation for Eva and some bottle-feeding for Wolfie, the small family was soon on the way to recovery.

The weekend after we'd found Eva and Wolfie, while they were still in intensive care at the vet, we delivered Two Spot and Zero to Katie. We crossed all of Manhattan and most of Brooklyn to bring them to her, an hour in the car with two mute kittens and two quiet humans.

Katie met us outside of the row house where she lived. She led us up the stairs to a nicely decorated apartment she rented on the second floor. The white walls, appealing art, and quirky secondhand furniture created a quiet haven that would be perfect for the kittens. Like the boys' room at Matt's house, Katie's bedroom was flooded with light coming in from a row of windows. As I'd suggested, Katie had set up her minuscule bathroom with food and a litter box. It would be better, I'd explained, that they spend their first couple of days in a small, enclosed space where they could get used to the sounds and smells of their new life. They weren't brave Number Threes. They needed some time to adapt.

When we opened the carrier that held both of them, neither moved. Matt and I had expected to hang around a little bit, but now we couldn't leave until they came out. We all three waited in anticipation in the bathroom for fifteen minutes until Matt decided that Katie and I should step out while he tried to coax them a little.

I knelt down on the tiles and reached in to give my two boys a scratch, guilt stricken for putting them through these frightening, though necessary, changes. Peering inside the carrier, I looked into Zero's beautiful eyes, massive disks in his pure white, babyish face. Ever the littlest of the lot, there were still traces in his face of the wild, bumbling kittens we'd first spotted three months earlier. I shifted my hand to Two Spot. With his sweet eagerness, he had secretly been my favorite. Every once in a while, I had let myself hope that Two Spot might not find a home so he could stay with me. Though each time I'd even considered the thought, I'd felt awful, because Zero needed his brother much more than I did. Two Spot, my darling little anime character with his massive ears, stared with confusion into my eyes. I loved this kitten, his quizzical expressions, his shy affection.

I pulled back my hand and stood up, leaving the room. After a bit of persuading and a little tugging, Matt got Two Spot and Zero to come out of the carrier. Matt thought everything was set for two days of slow transition to the new home. But then, as he slipped out the bathroom door, the kittens zipped by Matt and Katie, running and hiding immediately under the bed. Ever the escape artists.

I knelt down on the side of the bed, peering into the darkness. "Two Spot? Zero? Come on, babies."

I could see them huddled together along the back wall. On the other side of the bed, I saw Katie's head appear as she knelt down, too.

"Oh, Jasper and Theo, you clever boys," Katie murmured.

I was startled, affronted, hearing those names. But by using them, I understood that Katie had been thinking about the pair a great deal and was eager to accept them as hers.

"Don't worry, I've got some yummy food for you," she soothed them in a gentle voice.

The kittens were now Katie's responsibility, her rescue project. She would give them the patience and coaxing these two special beings needed.

There was nothing left for Matt and me to do. Katie thanked us again as she walked us down the stairs.

"I feel lucky to have found them," she said, as she shook our hand at the door. "Thank you for entrusting them to me." A real leave-taking.

We waved to her as we drove away. At the end of the block, I started crying, shoulder-shaking heaves wrenching from the middle of my chest. I couldn't stop during the next hour as we made our way up through New York traffic to Harlem, to have dinner with our friends Erik and Gail, the matchmakers who had brought Matt and me together. Had that party taken place just two years earlier? After all we'd been through, I felt as if I'd known this quiet, calm man beside me forever.

Matt kept his hand on my thigh the whole time, letting me grieve. I knew the kittens would be loved for the beings they were, all three of them. I knew they'd be happier with their own humans, their own homes, rather than having just a bit of our time each day. But those logical reassurances didn't matter. My heart was breaking. In leaving behind Two Spot and Zero that day, I was relinquishing a piece of myself, a part of my life I would never recapture. A time when my boyfriend and I sat in a sunny office, enchanted by three little kittens as we five beings worked to understand and trust one another.

The following week, Wolfie and Eva came home to us. We worked together to nurture these two delicate animals. All that fall, we administered Eva's twice-daily regimen of B12 shots, probiotics, antibiotics, and steroids. After bringing her back from the brink, we realized that now these two rescues needed to be adopted out. We were back on the treadmill. We also understood what a great team we had become as a couple, how much responsibility we'd come to feel for our neighborhood cats. We were now equipped as rescuers and ready to do what we could together.

We kept right on rescuing. During the following four years, Matt and I trapped and fostered nonstop, starting with Hanna's colony. We helped found the local group that provided trapping training with Carol McNichol, ran workshops, lent a hand to other folks in Jersey City and Hoboken, and spent tens of thousands of dollars on vet bills. In 2010, we brought Oona inside because I couldn't stand worrying a moment longer about her crossing the street or shivering out in the snow. Oona will always be wild at heart, ducking under the bed at the slightest noise and leaping out of your arms when you manage, through stealthy maneuvering, to pick her up. But though she misses the outdoors, spending hours staring out the window at the birds, I think she's accepted the trade-off. Maybe I'm fooling myself because I can't stand the idea of her back out there, on her own again. Yet, the few times she escaped out the front door, looking as shocked as we were that she was back out on the pavement, she hid under a car and meowed and meowed and meowed at us until we managed to sweet talk her into coming back inside. Because she loves us—and we love her. She chirps to me during the day, jumping up on the desk next to me and collapsing into a purring white heap. At night, as soon as we lie down in bed, she springs up to sit by our side, rubbing her head against our hands. We didn't tame her. We never could have. She chose to become part of our family.

We would have taken in more cats, done more, but in 2009 we had a little girl, a baby I never expected to have. Every single day, I think how lucky I am to have this joyful being in my life, to be part of her voyage of discovering the world around her, of seeing life through her amused, marveling, compassionate eyes. I never believed I could shoulder the responsibility of a child before Matt and the kittens. Everything Matt and I went through together showed me that, in fact, I could. Or actually, that we could. I would fail at times, make mistakes, maybe even drop the baby or a kitten one or two times. But it would be okay in the end. I was strong enough and grounded enough in the world and the people around me to work through the bad moments and revel in the good. Because I had Matt and his accepting commitment of everything I was to back me up. I loved Matt before the cats, but our project helped me see how we could work to understand each other and build a life together. I watched him accept my fears about making decisions, about being responsible for other beings. I came to understand that when he said he was a misanthrope, it was because he cared about the world so much that it made him a little bit of an outsider.

Caring about these kittens and their mother helped propel me toward the most common and daunting project I'd ever undertaken: figuring out what I truly want from life. For a long time, it was an endeavor I worked hard to avoid, taking advantage of distractions like work, alcohol, or just a whole lot of TV. But I learned with Matt how I could come to understand someone and love him even more deeply by tackling together a responsibility that seemed too much to handle on my own. I came to understand the importance of balance for my own well-being. Which is why I also didn't go to the other extreme and quit my job to become a full-time rescuer. Rescuing urban cats is one of the hardest emotional tasks I ever took on. There are always more ferals to fix, kittens to tame, horror stories about animal abuse to deal with. Cats live dark lives a lot of the time, on the edge of getting sick, dying outside in the cold, or being killed by a car, with kittens as adorable points of relief. But at times, even the sweetest kittens weigh on you, because they represent the struggle you're up against. The only way to stay sane is to have a community of cat people you can call and other interests you care about. Oh, and to watch a lot of funny cat videos.

So I kept working at *BusinessWeek*. But it became my job, not my life. I took days off to take cats to the vet. I continued leaving at normal hours. Matt and I traveled to Italy, France, and Mexico, we went skiing, we planned our wedding at my parents' farm in Virginia, and we became giddy parents. Then, when *BusinessWeek* was sold in 2009, one more established print publication upended by the Internet, I left to become a freelance writer, happily embracing a freedom and sense of self-reliance I would never have been at ease with before my adventures in New Jersey. And Tony and Pat even came to embrace TNR, working with us to fix their cats and find homes for their kittens.

Little by little, against my will, this street in Union City, with its dilapidated row houses and collection of oddball characters, drew me in. The community I needed—the one that accepted my foibles, gave me the room I never gave myself—found me when I was doing something I cared about. The evenings I spent sitting in a white plastic chair bathed in the blue haze of a bug zapper outlining our rescue plans for my neighbor Juan or discussing conspiracy theories with Carlo, the perpetual motion machine who owned the garage two doors down, bound me to this place. The cat people and all the frantic calls, the late-night texts strategizing about a trapping or a recently found litter, the time spent swapping war stories connected me to something other than my everyday cares.

We never thought of ourselves as crazy cat people, but over the course of ten years, we fixed sixty-five ferals and found homes for seventy friendly adults and kittens. We could only have done it with the support of our community. We could have devoted ourselves to anything, but for us in Union City, it turned out to be strays. The cats slinking by the deli down the road. The kittens living under a red truck in the parking lot across the street. The cats in Hanna's colony. Urban felines have a hard life. But we understand a little what it feels like to be outsiders looking for a place in this world.

Heather Green is a freelance writer and former journalist. For twelve years, she covered the Internet and digital media for *Business-Week*, winning prizes including the New York Press Club Crystal Gavel Award and the Front Page Award from the Newswomen's Club of New York. She wrote numerous cover stories on subjects from social media to e-commerce, pioneered the use of blogs, podcasts, and Twitter at *BusinessWeek*, and appeared on national and international TV stations, including CNN, CNBC, and the BBC. Prior to *BusinessWeek*, she worked for Bloomberg's financial newswire, where she launched their Internet beat, and at the *International Herald Tribune* in Paris. She has a B.A. from the University of Virginia and a graduate degree from the Institut d'Études Politiques de Paris. *To Catch a Cat* is her first book.

ABOUT THE AUTHOR

Photo © 2015 Marius Gabriel

Marius Gabriel served his author apprenticeship as a student at Newcastle University, where, to finance his postgraduate research, he wrote thirty-three Mills & Boon romances under a pseudonym. His identity as a man had to be kept secret until he turned to longer fiction under his own name. Gabriel is the author of eight sagas and historical novels, including the bestsellers *The Mask of Time*, *The Original Sin* and *The Seventh Moon*, and was once accused by *Cosmopolitan* magazine of 'keeping you reading while your dinner burns'. He very seldom burns his own, however, being an enthusiastic cook, as well as an artist and a musician. Born in South Africa in 1954, he has lived and worked in many countries, and now divides his time between London and Cairo. He has three grown-up children.